D0146339

Mackenzie

Mackenzie

A political biography
of William Lyon Mackenzie

John Sewell

James Lorimer & Company Ltd., Publishers
Toronto, 2002

James Lorimer & Company Ltd., acknowledges the support of the Ontario Arts Council. We acknowledge the support of the Government of Canada through the Book Publishing Industry Development Programs (BPIDP) for our publishing activities. We acknowledge the support of the Canada Council for the Arts for our publishing program.

Book Design: Nick Shinn

National Library of Canada Cataloguing in Publication

Sewell, John, 1940-
    Mackenzie : a political biography of William Lyon Mackenzie / author, John Sewell.

Includes bibliographical references and index.
ISBN 1-55028-767-2

    1. Mackenzie, William Lyon, 1795-1861. 2. Politicians—Canada—Biography. 3. Canada—Politics and government—1791-1841.
I. Title.

FC451.M33S49 2002   971.03'8'092   C2002-903999-1
F1032.M14S49 2002

James Lorimer & Company Ltd., Publishers
35 Britain St.
Toronto, Ontario
M5A 1R7
www.lorimer.ca

Printed and bound in Canada

Contents

Acknowledgments 5

1 In the Cemetery 7

2 Mackenzie's Early Years in Scotland 13

3 Mackenzie the Publisher 38

4 Mackenzie Enters the Assembly 63

5 Mackenzie's Elections and Ejections 85

6 Mackenzie, First Mayor of Toronto 106

7 Grievances Unresolved 121

8 The Rebellion Fails 139

9 Exile and Decline 163

10 Mackenzie's Political Ideas in Today's World 179

11 L'Envoi 201

Afterword: Searching for Mackenzie in Scotland 213

Endnotes 223

Bibliography 235

Index 243

To my son Nick

Acknowledgments

MY THANKS TO Alan Broadbent for his support during the research and writing of this book, and to the Ontario Arts Council for the grant which allowed me to pursue research in Scotland. John Fraser, Master of Massey College, kindly arranged for me to use a carrel at Massey College, where I essayed yet another draft of the manuscript.

Allison Savaria, my assistant for almost two decades, provided much help in sorting through and ordering the voluminous material (including excerpts from the *Colonial Advocate*) and deserves much thanks for this and other endeavours over the years. Diane Young was (thank goodness) persistent in helping shape the material into a coherence that I had not previously foreseen. Jim Lorimer offered encouragement along the whole process. Barbara Czarnecki's editing greatly improved the manuscript — thank you. I very much appreciate Ron Stagg's very useful comments on the manuscript, although I must own up to whatever errors and deficiencies remain. My wife, Liz Rykert, was absolutely terrific in supporting and challenging me at all the right moments.   —*Toronto, March 2002*

1 · In the Cemetery

IT'S THE PERFECT kind of day to be sitting beside a gravestone. Late October in Toronto, bright sun in a blue sky, yellow, red, and brown leaves loosened from their branches by a gentle breeze, falling into the cemetery. *Leav'd in October blood* is how Dylan Thomas put it, and it crackles under one's footstep.

I'm beside your grave, William Lyon Mackenzie. There's no expectation on my part of anything extraterrestrial or reincarnate. I've come here only because I could think of no better place to get a clear focus on you.

Here's the gravestone which the groundskeeper of this Necropolis swears was erected soon after your death in

1861. It looks too new, too fresh after almost a century and a half of Toronto winters, but he says that's a sign of how well a hard grey granite weathers the elements. The corners of the stone remain crisp, the rune engravings in the Celtic cross reaching the best part of twelve feet into the air are still fresh, the many names embossed on the faces of the stone are clear.

There's nothing religious about this marking. It feels perfunctory, almost without emotion. A hundred yards away is the memorial to your compatriots Samuel Lount and Peter Matthews, hanged for their leadership role in the 1837 rebellion. They lie beneath a broken column erected more than fifty years after their bodies were cut down from the gallows by Toronto Street. That stone exudes an aurora of sacrifice for the cause of democracy; it is inspiring.

Here's your grave, two plots in from the path, shaded by a silver birch. The name Lindsey is apparent first, Mackenzie not revealing itself unless approached from the awkward directions of east or north. The names and dates of death of your wife, Isabel, and some of your children — Barbara, Helen, Elizabeth, and George — are also on the stone along with those of your son-in-law Charles Lindsey and his children and descendants, and of one Wanda Gzowski, who married into the family, living as recently as 1989.

The more I learn about you, the more this common, perfunctory, and easy-to-overlook memorial makes sense. You are best known as the failed leader of the Rebellion of 1837, but that's hardly a fair marker of your life. You did little to polish your image for posterity, usually attending to the issues at hand, sometimes forgetting about securing an adequate perspective, but feverishly working away at a bevy of important causes. "Push, push, push for change" might have been employed as a marker for you, but it wasn't. There's nothing that identifies this stone with your life's work.

Perhaps that would be superfluous. Bill Kilbourn called you a firebrand and "an eccentric wholly seized with a public passion." Rick Salutin noted in the 1970s that you "continue to this day to inspire the most vehemently partisan assessments." Frederick Armstrong ascribed an extraordinary jumble of conflicting adjectives and phrases to you: "mercurial ... less than impressive ... loved to do battle ... failed to grasp the opportunities at hand ... fearless and at times foolhardy ... a reformed roué ... a Persistent Hero ... never held a decided policy ... constitutionally incapable of running the day-to-day business of government ... a blaze of colour ... a public nuisance ... of intemperate conduct ... vociferous ... a vast amount of drivel flowed from your pen ... a genuine folk hero."

To all these descriptions, many would append the word "radical."

Today, I suspect most would describe you as an ideologue ranting against the Family Compact. That's been my shorthand for you: a necessary hero in spite of your limitations.

Perhaps I took too literally Dennis Lee's poem :

Mackenzie was a crazy man
He wore his wig askew,
He donned three bulky overcoats
In case the bullets flew.
Mackenzie talked of fighting
While the fight went down the drain
But who will speak for Canada?
Mackenzie, come again.

The price of fame is such simplification.

As I have discovered, none of this is much help in understanding the struggle for which you became renowned, the struggle for responsive, responsible government in Upper Canada. The attention on the personal detail leads away from the thrust of your life's work; it distracts rather than illuminates. (Just to settle the question of the old wig you wore, it was not an affectation: when a child, you lost your hair from scarlet fever, and the wig attempted to restore an appearance of normalcy.) I've turned to you in the hope that your experiences will provide better understanding of the times in which I'm living, when responsive, responsible government itself seems under assault.

With the millennium just turned, I fear — and I am not alone in this fear — that the essence of democracy is disappearing from our political system. Just what that essence is, is not clear at first blush. Did university courses forget to convey the elements of democracy, assuming they were self-evident? Books I turn to glow

about "democracy" but don't define what they mean by
the word. It's not clear to me exactly what's being lost,
although I know something is dreadfully amiss.

Some doubters suggest that complainers like me are
just afraid of change or unwilling to embrace it with the
enthusiasm required. Others say democracy is as lively as
ever, and that our complaint is simply that interests other
than our own are now being attended to, and our unex-
pressed concern is loss of majority status. These excuses
have not rung true with me, yet I've had trouble putting
my finger on what the problem is. We have elections,
great bundles of civil rights, a free press. So what is lack-
ing in our political system that makes some of us think
we're heading away from democracy?

I've turned to you, Mackenzie, for hints about answers.
What was your fight all about? What did you see as the
basic elements needed for good government? Are those
elements present today, close to two centuries later?

I've tried to get past the forest of adjectives with which
your life has since been burdened and instead have
searched for what you wrote or speeches you gave that
were recorded. It's a voluminous record, but there are
many nuggets — occasionally great stretches, large
clumps of paragraphs — that bear directly on these questions. Mostly you were writing for your newspapers,
reflecting the issues of the moment without time to
address the structural underpinnings of your thought. But
there's a surprising consistency of approach in your writings, and the underlying set of principles you called on to

make sense of your world emerges. Those principles are large and lasting enough to also help define the issues of today.

Standing here on this fine fall day by your gravestone, I'm realizing one of the uses of history: to get a better fix on today's events, to find a context. One of my contemporaries, Vaclav Havel, a dissident in Eastern Europe released from jail a decade ago to become the president of the Czech Republic, writes, "the real test of a man is not how well he plays the role he has invented for himself, but how well he plays the role that destiny has assigned to him." The role destiny assigned you has been a matter of some conjecture, hence the differing views of how well you performed. But as I have learned — almost to my surprise — the role you played in defining the critical elements of a democratic society is extraordinarily powerful. Your voice still speaks strongly today. It clarifies the present and helps chart a course for the future.

2 · Mackenzie's Early Years in Scotland

WILLIAM LYON MACKENZIE came to Upper Canada in 1820, when he was twenty-five years old. His formative years were spent in Scotland and England, but it remains somewhat unclear exactly what he did in those years or how that early experience prepared him for his tumultuous life in Upper Canada.

In 1824, as his political opinions became widely known with the publication of his newspaper the *Colonial Advocate*, Mackenzie was challenged by members of the established order concerning his loyalty to the Crown. He responded by telling a story of his early life which confirms his loyalty, a story which is mostly plausible but which explains little and perhaps omits considerable detail that would have provided a more accurate and certainly more interesting picture, although less convincing on the loyalty issue. As he told it at that time, Mackenzie had no interest in journalism or politics until after he reached Upper Canada in 1820; then those passions sprang, *ex nihilo*, into his life. The first twenty-five years of his life, according to his telling, did nothing to prepare him for the powerful role he played from the first issue of the *Colonial Advocate* until he led the Rebellion of 1837. In retrospect it's not too convincing a narrative.

Mackenzie's version was later augmented by his son-in-law, Charles Lindsey, in his "official" biography, and then repeated and added to by other authors. But was there a more interesting story that Mackenzie didn't want to talk about once he had arrived in Upper Canada? Did he have something to hide, something which the Family Compact and others who supported the established order in Upper Canada could have used, if they had known, to discredit him? Perhaps.

Mackenzie was born in Dundee, Scotland, on March 12, 1795, and his father, who owned a small weaving enterprise, died three weeks later. He was brought up by his widowed mother, Elizabeth, who, though poor, had enough money and contacts to ensure that Mackenzie received a good education and a strong religious upbringing.

"My mother feared God," he said, "and He did not forget or forsake her; never in my early years can I recollect that divine worship was neglected in our little family when health permitted; never did she in family prayer forget to implore that He who doeth all things well, would establish in righteousness the throne of our monarch, setting wise and able counsellors around it." He then continued brilliantly to use this kindly scene as his defence against the accusation of siding with a radical cause: "Was it from the precept, was it from the example of such a mother and such relations," Mackenzie asked somewhat hyperbolically, "that I was to imbibe that disloyalty, democracy, falsehood, and deception, with which my writings are by the government editor charged? Surely not."

Mackenzie started his working career in 1814 as a shopkeeper. His shops failed and he headed south, spending at least a year or two in London, either working at dull but respectable jobs or drinking and gambling, depending on which version of the official story you believe. In April 1820 he emigrated to Canada.

In his first four years in Canada, Mackenzie tried a variety of ventures to establish himself and his family. Then in 1824, he began publishing the *Colonial Advocate*. With its launch, the course of political life in Upper Canada changed forever. Mackenzie immediately became the voice of Reform politics, a loose coalition of interests that opposed the colonial regime and advocated responsible government. By 1828 he would be elected to the Legislative Assembly, and the Reformers would achieve a clear majority there. Unlike anyone else, Mackenzie made all the difference in the tone and direction of Upper Canada politics.

It seems extraordinary that Mackenzie could have had such a powerful influence without some previous experience with either newspaper publishing or politics. Of course, the Family Compact would not have been reassured to learn that Mackenzie already knew how to publish a newspaper supporting the Reform agenda. Nor would he have aided his cause by talking about his political experience. Better to disavow knowledge of the British Radicals across the ocean and the events they organized, and say, as he did, "We have never been disloyal subjects nor radical reformers; we have neither joined Spa-field mobs, nor benefited by the harangues of Hunt, Cobbett and Watson." He may not have attended the famous Spa meeting in England in 1816. He may never have heard Henry Hunt, William Cobbett or William Watson speak — all three addressed numerous gatherings in England and Scotland, where he would have had the opportunity to do so. He certainly knew who they were.

Many records were destroyed as Mackenzie fled the failed rebellion in 1837, and the remaining records in Scotland are scanty. Nevertheless, there are abundant clues to what Mackenzie probably did before coming to Canada. Scottish politics engulfed many young men from the mid-eighteenth century on.

Bonnie Prince Charlie's defeat at Culloden in 1756 was a serious blow to the progressive political movement in Scotland, but it did not put an end to the hope for change. Prince Charles fled to France, and that country became a haven for Scottish dissent and dissenters. The French

Revolution in 1789 was strongly supported by many of those active in Scottish politics, particularly as the rough hand of the enclosure movement produced so much hardship in the last decades of the eighteenth century. Crofter families living in cottages were summarily evicted as large estates were created to support sheep for the production of wool, and this pressure was fuel to the cause of reform.

Dundee, where Mackenzie was born, was a hotbed of political activity. In 1790, for example, Dundee's Whig Club sent a message of congratulation on the revolution to the French National Assembly. In 1792 the Dundee Friends of Liberty planted a tree of liberty in the High Street and forced the lord provost to march around it while tipping his hat. That year saw many demonstrations in Dundee on behalf of liberty, and finally English troops were called out to break them up. The government pressed charges of sedition for the organizers of the protests, convicted several men, and transported them to Australia.

Britain declared war against France in 1793 in the hope of restoring the French king, and that provoked even more anti-war protest. "The seeds of socialism and nationalism, the two dominant political ideologies in Dundee today," wrote one author in reference to this period, "had been sown. The defeat of the United Scotsmen and the repression that followed drove the Dundee radicals underground, and they turned their attention to organizing the early trade unions, also illegal under the anti-combination laws."

That organizing occurred over the next two decades. Alexander Richmond, a weaver from Glasgow, called meetings of weavers to push for a basic wage, successfully organizing a society of weavers' unions with a local in virtually every town, including Dundee. A court case was brought in 1812, confirming a common employment contract for weavers, but the employers refused to honour the decision. A strike in early 1813 across Scotland was broken after nine weeks.

The Radical cause was supported throughout England and Scotland in journals such as the *Edinburgh Review* (which Mackenzie read regularly), *The Black Dwarf*, and the *Weekly Political Register* published by the influential English journalist William Cobbett. The *Dundee, Perth and Cupar Advertiser* was a vehicle for progressive politics from the time it was first published in 1801, and its editor from 1811 to 1825 was Robert Stephen Rintoul, nicknamed "Radical Rinty." Dundee was a particular locus of parliamentary reform, given that it did not have its own representation but had to select, in conjunction with four other towns, one member to sit in Parliament in distant London.

Mackenzie's early brush with the cause of reform apparently occurred before he was fifteen years of age. His was a familiar face in the premises of the *Dundee Advertiser* in the first few years, when Rintoul was the "free-thinking editor" of a paper with strong Radical political views. It is said that Mackenzie used the paper's reading room, and it seems unlikely that this would have occurred without the newspaper's politics rubbing off, or without his learning how a newspaper was put together. Articles and reports for the paper were filed anonymously or under a pseudonym, making it impossible today to know the names of different writers, even though copies of the paper are still available. The administrative records of the paper are no longer extant. Mackenzie's precise relationship to the paper and to Rintoul are unknown.

At about the same time as Rintoul took over the *Advertiser,* in 1811, Mackenzie became a founding member of the Dundee Rational Institution, a club concerned with intellectual discussion and debate about scientific matters but apparently with little political involvement. It probably also served as a lending library for its members. He became librarian and secretary, responsible for minutes of meetings and correspondence, and he may have been the author of a booklet titled "The Laws and Regulations of the Dundee Rational Institution." The booklet, published in 1813 when Mackenzie was eighteen years old, outlines a theme that would dominate Mackenzie's public life: the advantages of public discussion to clarify ideas and individual opinions.

Much advantage too may be derived from discussions: They will enable the members to arrange their ideas with order, and to deliver them readily and in accurate language; and they will promote the grand object of their study, — the discriminating of truth and falsehood. As every member's observations will be submit-

ted to the scrutiny of others, he will be guarded against
that dogmatism and prejudice in favour of his own
opinions which but too frequently lower the dignity and
impair the usefulness of solitary students.

This may be a very early example of Mackenzie's writing. The title page of the booklet lists the publisher as
Robert Stephen Rintoul.

There are other links between Mackenzie and Rintoul.
A 1901 centenary publication of the *Dundee Advertiser*
includes an article on Rintoul's editorship listing Rintoul's
five closest friends, noting them as recognized leaders of
liberal opinion. One friend is Francis Jeffrey, publisher of
the *Edinburgh Review*. The first issue of the *Colonial
Advocate*, published on May 18, 1824, lists a number of
people to whom Mackenzie promises to send free copies
of the paper, including "Francis Jeffrey, Esq. Edinburgh."
Rintoul's influence on Mackenzie's paper was noticed
by others. A subscriber to the *Colonial Advocate* wrote
Mackenzie in 1825 to say how much the paper reminded
him of Rintoul's *Dundee Advertiser*. When Mackenzie
returned to Britain in 1832, he made a point of meeting
with Rintoul, who had since become editor of the
Spectator. It's not unreasonable to believe that Mackenzie
learned newspaper publishing and reform-minded politics
from Rintoul.

Mackenzie's progressive political bent was also encouraged through his connection with the Lesslie family.
Edward Lesslie was a successful shopkeeper in Dundee

as well as an acknowledged liberal, and he knew Mackenzie through the Dundee Rational Institution, of which he was also a member. It is possible that Edward Lesslie provided the initiative and capital for the general store which Mackenzie opened in 1814 in Alyth, a small town a dozen miles outside Dundee. When it failed in 1816 during a severe economic downturn, Lesslie was responsible for handling bankruptcy sales, and he may have been helpful in Mackenzie's second attempt to set up a shop in Dundee the following year. A plaque marks its site in the Overgate district in the heart of the city. When Mackenzie left Scotland, Edward's eldest son, John, went with him. One source states that Edward Lesslie sent John to Canada to try his fortune, provided "with sufficient stock to commence business," and "accompanied by one of his father's employees by the name of William Lyon Mackenzie." (An 1831 entry in the diary of John's brother James Lesslie states that Mackenzie "was in my father's employ in Dundee." At that time James, who had emigrated to Canada in 1822, and Mackenzie were close politically: James was elected to Toronto city council in 1834 and nominated Mackenzie as mayor.)

The general political mood of both Britain and Scotland in the early nineteenth century was so uproarious that in 1816 the government suspended habeas corpus, the legal tool that defended people from arbitrary arrest by government authorities. Individuals such as Henry Hunt and William Cobbett travelled the country making provocative speeches to large crowds. Cobbett was forced to flee to

America to avoid arrest for sedition, not returning to England until November 1819, carrying with him the remains of the Radical hero Tom Paine (author of *The Rights of Man*) for burial.

In 1818 the Tories were re-elected with a majority in Parliament, and they made it clear that reform was not on the agenda, but the outside pressure for change intensified. In July 1819 about thirty thousand people gathered for a Radical meeting in Paisley, a centre of the weaving trade just outside of Glasgow. The next month sixty thousand gathered at St. Peter's Square in Manchester to advocate change, but they were attacked by pro-government forces. Many were injured and eleven people were killed in what was called "Peterloo," a reference to the battle of Waterloo. "The country," remarked one scholar, "was on the brink of revolution."

More agitation and many large demonstrations followed. In Dundee ten thousand people attended a meeting at the Magdalene Yards in November 1819 to protest the massacre at Peterloo and to demand "one man, one vote." George Kinloch, the Radical laird, spoke at this demonstration and was arrested for sedition. He fled to France in December just before his trial began, not returning to Dundee until 1823, when charges against him were stayed. Kinloch was such a local hero that in 1832, after passage of the great Reform Bill, he was elected as the first member of Parliament for Dundee.

In January 1820 King George III died and was succeeded by the debauched and hated George IV, who also opposed reform. The Cato Street conspiracy, an aborted attempt to overthrow the government, was discovered in early February 1820, and questions were raised about how it might be linked to radical political actions in other centres. In Scotland the demand was for parliamentary independence, and a group was formed which was determined to create a provisional government.

The Scottish group planned an uprising for early April in Glasgow, although by mid-March government spies organized by the home secretary, Lord Sidmouth, had infiltrated the group and had (unbeknownst to almost everyone involved) arrested some of those intending to hold positions of power in the provisional government. Nevertheless, the rebels posted a proclamation in Glasgow and in neighbouring towns on April 1 which read, in part:

The numerous Public Meetings held throughout the Country have demonstrated to you that the interest of all Classes are the same. That the production of the Life and Property of the Rich Man is the interest of the Poor Man, and in return, it is the interest of the Rich to protect the Poor from the iron grip of DESPOTISM, for, when its victims are exhausted in the lower circles, there is no assurance but that its ravages will be continued in the upper. For once set in motion, it will continue to move till a succession of Victims fall.

Our principles are few, and founded on the basis of our Constitution which was purchased with the Dearest Blood of our Ancestors, and which we swear to transmit to posterity unsullied, or perish in the Attempt. Equality of Rights (not of Property) is the object for which we contend, and which we consider as the only security for our Liberties and Lives.

Rebels marched on Glasgow on Wednesday, April 5. The *Glasgow Herald,* which had given the proclamation wide currency, on April 7 reported on gatherings of Radicals (with flags, drums, and pistols) in nearby Bridgeton and Calton. It noted that several dozen Radicals marched through Conderrat and engaged the government cavalry at Bonnybridge, and that "between Tuesday night and Wednesday morning, the smiths' shops in said village were taken possession of by the Radicals, who, after stuffing the windows with turf, etc., so as to prevent the sound of their hammers being heard, fell to work making pikes and such infernal instruments." The paper said that "on Tuesday, about one o'clock, a detachment of between 12 and 16 Radicals, supposed to be from Paisley, well furnished with fire-arms and other offensive weapons, visited the house of Mr. Buchanan, farmer, near Pollokshaws, on a search for arms," and that government troops were in a state of alert. In fact, the Glasgow uprising was put down within a day, but insurgent activity continued for almost a week in nearby centres.

On Monday, April 10, the *Herald* reported that the insurrection had spread to Greenock, the other significant port on the Clyde. Five prisoners were taken there because the Paisley jail was full, but a crowd gathered, a fight with government forces ensued, with three people killed and eighteen injured. That evening the crowd reconvened, broke into the jail and freed the five prisoners.

Nearly a hundred participants were charged with high treason, but many of those who were charged fled the country. The captured leaders were found guilty and executed; others were transported to Australia. The Scottish insurrection of 1820 was effectively quashed.

There are no documents which tie Mackenzie to the insurrection or any other Scottish political activity, but there are tantalizing possibilities. Of most interest is the fact that Mackenzie was, by his own account, in Glasgow in April 1820, sailing to Canada on a ship called *Psyche*. (Although there is no record of such a boat arriving at or leaving from either Glasgow or Greenock in April or in the months on either side, it seems not unreasonable to accept his word. It is generally thought that port records for that period captured only a portion of the port traffic.)

What was Mackenzie doing in the Glasgow area during or just after the uprising? There is no record of any previous visit to Glasgow. Was he involved in these events in some minor capacity, and did he feel compelled to leave quickly in fear of arrest? One author claims Mackenzie travelled regularly between York and Glasgow, "keeping the English and Scottish Radicals in touch with each other," and he fled "like hundreds of other young Radicals," but this claim is unsubstantiated. A significant evidentiary problem is that Lord Sidmouth's spies had so infiltrated the rebels' ranks that some historians think *agents provocateurs* may have played a more considerable role than the rebels themselves. This would have given a strong incentive for government agents to destroy whatever records had existed. It seems unlikely that more detail will be uncovered about the 1820 insurrection.

Why did Mackenzie not set out for Canada from a port near London, or from Dundee? One author puts him in Dundee in late November 1819, just at the time Kinloch was speaking at the rally that led to his arrest. The organizing in Dundee was part of the same movement as in the Glasgow area. It seems that Mackenzie had chosen to be in Glasgow at this time. Since there were no previous hints that emigration to Canada was in his plans, embarking on the *Psyche* was a decision made in the moment.

A further question centers on the eighteen months Mackenzie claims to have spent in dissolute behaviour in London in 1818 and 1819. Lindsey is skeptical in describing this period of Mackenzie's life — although he seems to have shaved three or four years from Mackenzie's age, given that he was born in 1795 — writing, "He confessing to having ... plunged in to the vortex of dissipation and contracted a fondness for play. But all at once he abandoned the dangerous path on which he had entered, and after the age of twenty-one [four?] never played a game of cards. A more temperate man than he was for the rest of his life, it would have been impossible to find."

"Dissipation" had a sudden onset and then an equally sudden disappearance. It's not the kind of dissipation that affects many individuals, and maybe the tale is nothing more than Mackenzie's cover for a period of subversive political activity.

The claim of a dissolute life must be placed beside another, also advanced by Mackenzie for the same period in London. After a short stint as a bookkeeper for the Kennet and Avon canal company, he said he worked as a clerk for Lord Lonsdale. This seems most unlikely, since both William Lowther, first earl of Lonsdale (1757–1844) and William Lowther, second earl of Lonsdale (1787–1872) were staunch Tories and members of the government, the former holding the position of lord of the admiralty (beginning in 1810) and lord of treasury. It seems extraordinarily unlikely that someone with such powerfully progressive roots would agree to work with the Tories — or that they in turn would retain someone so out of tune with the Tory cause at a time of such political ferment. No record of Mackenzie's employment with Lord Lonsdale has been found. Did this employment ever occur, or did Mackenzie claim a Tory connection as another form of cover story?

During the putative London period, Mackenzie later wrote, he also made a trip to France to deliver a letter of some kind to Duc de La Rochefoucault-Liancourt. The duke was culturally progressive, supporting the causes of science and education, but he was a well-known and powerful establishment figure, appointed by Louis XVI as president of the Estates General, and he remained loyal to the king during the revolution. His loyalty forced him into exile in the United States in 1792; he returned in 1799.

One can understand Mackenzie enjoying a discussion
with the duke — Mackenzie was forever curious — but
what was this trip, undocumented except for Mackenzie's
own account, all about? Did Mackenzie mention the duke's
name as a way of again showing loyalty to the Crown?
The reasons most Scots visited France at this time were to
renew radical contacts and to seek relief from the repres-
sive English regime. Bonnie Prince Charlie and his follow-
ers sought refuge in France. Kinloch escaped to France to
avoid arrest. Perhaps Mackenzie was visiting France to
carry some message for Scottish Radicals?

One further piece of the puzzle: after leaving for
Canada, he did not return to Scotland for twelve years.
Instead of going back to seek a wife and to help his
mother join him in the new country where he was prosper-
ing financially, Mackenzie had his mother and prospective
bride come to him. In the circumstances it looks as though
he stayed abroad for a reason — possibly a political one.

As he sailed for the British Isles in 1832, reform was in
the air and even George Kinloch was about to be elected
to Parliament. Mackenzie may have met with Kinloch,
whom he knew from his Dundee days; certainly he noted
Kinloch's death in a dispatch to the *Advocate* in 1833,
saying Kinloch "did all he could to promote the welfare of
those for whom I was deputed to this country" and that
"in early youth I experienced strong proofs of his friendship." The words are telling: Mackenzie considered himself "deputed" to Upper Canada and linked his cause to
Kinloch's.

Dundee saw its share of rebellion while Mackenzie ran his shops. In 1816 a riot occurred there, resulting from an increase in the price of cornmeal, and the event had a political edge, with attempts to push for political change. The British government appointed an advocate to investigate the riot; the testimony of fifty or sixty witnesses does not include any mention of Mackenzie. The *Dundee Advertiser* reported on a meeting of reformers chaired by Kinloch on January 31, 1817, without naming other participants. The resulting petition to Dundee City Council asking support for a public meeting on parliamentary reform was signed by 110 persons and presented on February 7, 1817. It was destroyed in a fire in 1931. We will never know whether Mackenzie was a signatory. Newspaper reports of Kinloch's famous speech in Dundee in November 1819 do not name any others present.

So if Mackenzie started his career as a rebel in Scotland, the evidence no longer exists. Nevertheless, given his strong and effective activities in Upper Canada, it seems reasonable to believe that Mackenzie gained considerable political experience from these events in Scotland and England: experience in defining and popularizing the issues, organizing public meetings, mobilizing public support, writing and speaking. One can imagine why it was something he would not want to mention in 1824 since it could have discredited him as he pursued a progressive agenda in Upper Canada. Better to plant a few false clues. Later in life, in the midst of numerous tribulations, Mackenzie often cited events that had occurred earlier by way of justification or explanation. But this period of his life did not seem to be part of his memory later on: he left his words of 1824 unchallenged.

On the editorial side, as already noted, he had a passing acquaintance with the *Dundee Advertiser* and its editor, Robert Rintoul. The other serious editorial influence on him may have been William Cobbett. Cobbett was a leading figure in the political life of Britain. He began publishing the *Weekly Political Register* in 1802 (it continued until his death in 1835), and the next year he began to transcribe and publish parliamentary debates, which found a wide market. These transcriptions were edited by a man called T.C. Hansard, and the name stuck: virtually all records of parliamentary debates are today referred to as "Hansard." More than that, Cobbett shaped the English political culture in the decades before the great Reform Bill in 1832, in the same way Mackenzie shaped the political culture in Upper Canada before the rebellion.

Mackenzie visited Cobbett when he made his journey to England in 1832 and wrote: "He is evidently a man of an ardent temperament, of strong and powerful passions — and I believe his object is to increase the comforts and lessen the misery of the great body of the people, but it is evident he is not very scrupulous as to the means of bringing about this great good .... I should not be at all surprised if few find him not so great a democrat in the House of Commons as he is in the *Weekly Register*."

The statement begins in a complimentary fashion, only to conclude exuding faint praise, as though disappointment began to cloud over the encounter. There may be good reason. It's entirely possible that Cobbett was Mackenzie's hero, someone that Mackenzie tried to emulate, but when finally confronted in flesh and bone, Cobbett didn't quite measure up to Mackenzie's very high expectations.

There are some clues to support this conclusion, but not much hard evidence about what made Mackenzie follow the path he did in Upper Canada, from businessman to journalist and a leading voice of reform. As will be noted shortly, there were few role models in Canada or America for Mackenzie to follow, and there are many parallels to suggest that Cobbett may have been Mackenzie's distant mentor.

The men trod many similar paths although Cobbett was almost three decades older. Like Cobbett, Mackenzie printed (but did not transcribe) debates of the Legislative Assembly, one consequence of which (again similar to Cobbett's experience in London) was to provoke a motion of censure from Family Compact members for being so forward in his attempt to inform the public. Like Cobbett, Mackenzie was a journalist who wielded an enormous influence on the public by shaping issues and throwing light on the way political questions were viewed. Like Cobbett, Mackenzie shifted his views on many issues, so much so that one critic says his "policies were temporary expedients honestly arrived at, and discarded if no longer applicable." Like Cobbett for most of his life, Mackenzie was clearly on the side of reform and spoke for it at many

public gatherings. In the early 1820s Cobbett made a tour
of the English countryside, the result of which was his
most successful book, *Rural Rides*, describing the
changes industrialization was bringing to the British rural
tradition. Shortly after the book was published, Mackenzie
toured Upper Canada, apparently following Cobbett's
inspiration, and published his observations in 1825 in a
lengthy appendix to the *Colonial Advocate*. To escape
charges of sedition in 1817, Cobbett fled to the United
States for several years until the situation cooled down;
Mackenzie did the same following the rebellion in 1837.

Further to these parallels, many of the conclusions drawn
about Cobbett's life and influence seem to fit Mackenzie
in an admirable fashion. For instance, the sentiments of
E.P. Thompson in his monumental *The Making of the
English Working Class* could easily be ascribed to
Mackenzie:

> Cobbett throws his influence across the years from the
> end of the Wars until the passing of the Reform Bill. To
> say that he was in no sense a systematic thinker is not
> to say that his was not a serious intellectual influence.
> It was Cobbett who *created* this Radical intellectual cul-
> ture, not because he offered its most original ideas, but
> in the sense that he found the tone, the style, and the
> arguments which could bring the weaver, the school-
> master, and the shipwright, into a common discourse.
> Out of the diversity of grievances and interests he
> brought a Radical consensus. His *Political Registers*

were like a circulating medium which provided a common means of exchange between the experiences of men of widely differing attainments.

It would be fair to say that the *Colonial Advocate* had much the same impact in Upper Canada. Mackenzie helped to find the language to shape the issues, at a time when there was no road map to fall back on. The concepts of democracy and participation, which might be taken for granted as common knowledge (if not common belief) today, were not present in the 1820s and early 1830s.

Mackenzie played a large part in helping a common political culture of reform to emerge in Upper Canada, making good use of the *Colonial Advocate* and other publications.

And, like Cobbett, Mackenzie did not approach things from a theoretical point of view. He formed political opinions on the basis of experience and assumed that other reasonable people would come to the same conclusions. The result might not be consistency, but that was a small cost. "It is not difficult to show that Cobbett had some very stupid and contradictory ideas," writes Thompson, "and sometimes bludgeoned his readers with specious arguments. But such demonstrations are beside the point unless the profound, the truly profound, democratic influence of Cobbett's attitude to his audience is understood. [Tom] Paine anticipates the tone; but Cobbett, for thirty years, talked to his audience like this, until men were talking and arguing like Cobbett all over the land. He assumed, as a matter scarcely in need of demonstration, that every citizen whatsoever had the power of reason, and that it was by argument addressed to the common understanding that matters should be settled."

Mackenzie, too, created the language which sustained the cause of reform, and that language survived the many disagreements about some of the precise solutions he might be advocating.

The gains that experience produced for Cobbett — and Mackenzie — were offset by difficulties in providing leadership and making strategic decisions. Thompson continues, regarding Cobbett:

Deficient in theory he was also sometimes plainly mischievous in his immediate influence upon political strategy, while he was by no means always as straightforward in personal and public dealings as he asked other men to be. For his failings as a political leader he was not fully responsible. He was a journalist, and not a political leader or organizer, and it was only the accident of the context (the outlawing of effective political organization) which forced him into the other role. But, if he did not choose to be a political leader, he was (like other men in this predicament) reluctant to see the movement go in any way but the way which he prescribed. When all these — and other — failings are accounted, it is easy to underestimate him, as a nostalgic romantic or a bully.

These same flaws may be the nub of Mackenzie's failure to provide the leadership expected from him, particularly in 1837. The skill of popularizing the Reform agenda was entirely different than the skill of providing leadership under the extreme pressure of rebellion. He was imbued with the first skill but not, perhaps, the second.

In spite of these apparent similarities, nothing in Mackenzie's writings admits that Cobbett may have been a model for him. However, Mackenzie was an inveterate clipper of newspapers, and upon his death the clippings were sorted by his son-in-law and biographer Charles Lindsey. One set of clippings — thirty-eight items in all — deal with William Cobbett. Few of these items are Cobbett's own writings or from the *Weekly Political Register*, which Mackenzie must have had access to. Instead, most deal with the man himself: personal notes of the affectionate relationship between Cobbett and his wife; reports on libel trials Cobbett faced; criticisms of Cobbett; reports on Cobbett's character (including one with the note, in Mackenzie's handwriting, "Cobbett's bad conduct"); the report of the death of Cobbett's wife. Mackenzie clearly had a personal interest in Cobbett, who may well have provided an example for the kind of journalist and activist he wanted to be.

One item, noted in Mackenzie's handwriting as "Mr. Cobbett's memm [memorandum]," is a letter dated 1833 from Cobbett, apparently about the drafting of a petition. In all likelihood Cobbett scratched this during the meeting he and Mackenzie had in London that year:

> That the Governor of Upper Canada is so and so
> That the Council are such and such —
> That the powers of the Governor are —
> That the Council does this and that —
> That the Assembly is —
> That its powers are —
> That the grievances are as follows:
>> 1. That —
>> 2. —

It's unclear what purpose this advice served other than to confirm that the two shared at least a discussion on strategy, since Mackenzie had just filed a petition and list of grievances with the government in Britain. Also included is a clipping from the Weekly Political Register of June 12, 1817, underlined in Mackenzie's hand, in which Cobbett promises "never to become a citizen of America." The possibility of American citizenship tempted Mackenzie briefly after his expulsion in 1837; he resisted then but yielded in a moment of despair later in his exile. The file also includes a laudatory piece on Cobbett by the English writer William Hazlitt and a touching article, author unknown, of a visit to the birth and burial place of Cobbett in 1844, nine years after his death. In all, the collection of clippings demonstrates a great deal of affection on Mackenzie's part.

The parallels of the life trajectories of these two men are astounding. It would have been hard for Mackenzie to have missed the similarities, just as it would have been hard for him to pass up the opportunity of going to Cobbett's home in Kensington during his visit to London. Perhaps he saw it as a last chance to meet his role model. Mackenzie could hardly praise Cobbett publicly — that would have raised the same issues as if in 1824 he had mentioned his friendship with George Kinloch as proof of loyalty. (In fact, Mackenzie waited to praise Kinloch until after the Radical laird had been elected to Parliament and had safely died in 1833.) To be effective in Upper Canada it may have been critical that he keep the important influences in his past hidden.

At the end of the day, we have too few hard facts about Mackenzie's life before he came to Upper Canada. But it is fair to assume that he received excellent training for the roles he soon pursued.

3 · Mackenzie the Publisher

"ONE THING IS certain," Mackenzie wrote, "no free popular government can exist unless the people are informed. An ignorant Republic would surely degenerate into a most corrupt and hateful government." This was published a year before the Rebellion of 1837 erupted, but Mackenzie could very well have been heard to voice this opinion when he established his first newspaper, the *Colonial Advocate*, four years after he arrived in Upper Canada. The public availability of information was a matter of great concern to him throughout his life.

Mackenzie did not begin life in Upper Canada as a newspaper publisher. Arriving in North America in 1820,

probably at Quebec (there is no record of the *Psyche* harbouring at Quebec, although that is where Mackenzie said
he landed), he proceeded to Montreal, where he worked
for several weeks with the two skills he had learned in the
Old World: as a bookkeeper for the Lachine Canal (work
that must have been very similar to what he had done for
the Kennet and Avon canal company), and as a journalist
with the *Montreal Herald*. Within a few weeks he moved
to York, where he set up shop with Lesslie. York (later
Toronto) was a town of fifteen-hundred people, with a
large natural harbour and forested hinterland that offered
the opportunity of growth. The centre of government in
Upper Canada was established there. A fort had been
erected at the western entrance to the harbour, and it had
been rebuilt since being torched by American troops in
the invasion of 1812. The town, too, had recovered from
the ravages of that war, and a long period of immigration
and growth was underway.

York's main streets were Front and King, and many of
the town's buildings were located on them between Yonge
Street (laid out by the first Lieutenant Governor, John
Graves Simcoe, in the last decade of the eighteenth century) and Taddle Creek, which ran into the mouth of the
Don River. Mackenzie's shop was located on the south
side of King just east of Church Street, across from St.
James' Anglican Church, a wooden building which would
burn down in 1849 and be replaced by a larger church
more fitting to a cathedral status. The shop was run in
partnership with John Lesslie, his companion on the journey

to Canada, selling books and medicines. Capital for the enterprise probably came from John's father. The shop was a success, and a second was opened the following year in Dundas, a prosperous mill town sixty miles (and several days' ride) west of York, where Mackenzie then moved.

In June 1822, his mother, Elizabeth, arrived from Dundee. Mackenzie went to Montreal to meet her. She brought with her Mackenzie's eight-year-old natural son, James, whom she had raised. James was born in 1814 when Mackenzie ran a shop in Alyth; his mother was Isabel Reid. Accompanying them was a twenty-year-old woman from Dundee, Isabel Baxter, whom Elizabeth had selected as Mackenzie's wife. The two were married within three weeks, on July 1, 1822, in Montreal. It proved a long and successful marriage.

Mackenzie returned with his bride and family to Dundas, where he was either the store manager or a partner in the business. He experienced none of the financial problems he had had with storekeeping in Scotland. Here he prospered. But in 1823 the partnership came to an end. Either Lesslie forced a sale of Mackenzie's share in the business because Mackenzie, having married Isabel, had dropped his interest in marrying Lesslie's sister, or Mackenzie was denied a partnership and struck out on his own. In early 1824, he left Dundas and opened a shop in Queenston, near Niagara Falls. But the Queenston store was short-lived: he quickly sold the business and became a publisher, and in a few months he purchased a printing press of his own. He may have been influenced in this decision by his friend Robert Randall, who had been elected to the Legislative Assembly several years earlier.

The first issue of the *Colonial Advocate* appeared in May 1824, and in it Mackenzie stated his new, high-minded purpose: "We have made our election; it is to have only one patron, and that patron is the People — the people of the British Colonies." In 1831 he defined the purpose of his publishing endeavours as to "do the people's business and check and expose speculation and official knavery."

The newspaper business promised no security. Half a dozen other papers were then published in Upper Canada, and their financial success depended on regular government advertising, something Mackenzie made clear in his first issue he would never rely on. He resented establishment newspapers such as the *Western Mercury* from Hamilton, which he alleged was supported only by this kind of revenue, not by readership interest. He said that this paper was "openly in the pay of those who have sought for thirty years to keep the people in ignorance, squander the fruits of their patient industry, depress the humbler classes under colour of law, and unite their efforts to crush every man whether judge or labourer, farmer or printer, who had dared to stand up for the British constitution and the good of the country." He thought such papers existed as part of the patronage system, called their publishers sycophants, and bitterly said, "These mean fellows will bow and scrape, and fetch and carry, tell lies or babble nonsense, praise and flatter or abuse and scandalize, just as they are bid — nothing is too bad for them, so that they can get the means of existence...."

He chastised the *Mercury* as an organ of "a knot of petty magistrates, placemen, incorporated priests, and hungry office seekers, who would devour a province like a cloud of locusts if their power was at all equal to their inclinations."

The main portion of the revenues from the *Colonial Advocate*, according to Mackenzie's thinking, would come from subscriptions. The price was six pence per issue, and there were several dozen subscription agents throughout Upper Canada as well as a handful in Lower Canada, the United States, and Britain. He printed about a thousand copies of each issue, and for the first six months he published almost every week. But his political agenda overwhelmed the business agenda. Since Mackenzie saw the *Advocate* as a political tool, he sent it to many who were considered influential but did not subscribe. The postal service required quarterly postal payments in advance, which put considerable pressure on the business aspect of the enterprise.

The first issue listed more than two dozen eminent individuals who would be sent the paper at no charge, "and we shall continue to add to this list such names of public characters as from their situations or talents, in Britain or the United States, may be supposed to exercise an influence over public opinion in these countries, as well as in the Colonies." In addition to Francis Jeffrey of the *Edinburgh Review,* the eminent included the Duc de la Rochefoucault-Liancourt of France, and Daniel Webster in the United States.

The full title of the paper was the *Colonial Advocate and Journal of Agriculture, Manufactures & Commerce.* Like all good newspapers it promised to do more than simply report on political affairs, and it would have something for everyone. There was agricultural news and advice, world news often taken from other papers (publishers borrowed freely from one another since there were no firm rules about copyright), letters from readers who were rarely identified by name — again, the style of the day — and poems, particularly those of Robbie Burns. As a related business enterprise Mackenzie published books — more than a dozen in 1827, including a seed catalogue and a Methodist church report, and an annual *Poor Richard's Almanac,* with a print run of ten thousand copies. In 1827 he also became the official printer for the government of Upper Canada.

Mackenzie saw it as his role, as a publisher, to describe the actions of those who wielded power in Upper Canada, in the hope that the public could be informed and educated. "Far be it from us to desire to bring into disrepute the government of this country," Mackenzie wrote in the first issue of the *Colonial Advocate,* "yet we will not fail to point out their errors. Ridicule shall not be spared: it may effect our purpose when grave argument would fail." He continued, "We will carefully go over the principal matters connected with his [Lieutenant Governor Sir

Peregrine Maitland's] administration.... For the present we cannot remember anything he has done of a public nature worth recording."

That first issue touched on several issues that Mackenzie returned to again and again. He chastised the system of Clergy Reserves, which gave the Church of England one parcel of land for every six that went to settlers, and the idea of an established church. He complained about the small amount of power that residents of Upper Canada had to affect their own affairs, noting that England legislated for Upper Canadians "without the aid of one representative on our part to state our wants." He complained about the interests of those appointed to their positions of power, asking, "Have the members of our Legislative Council ever been other than the most obsequious, cringing, worshippers of power?"

In subsequent issues of the paper he dealt with other concerns that stayed with him for many years: the development of canals, whether from Burlington Bay to Lake Ontario (which he supported) or from Lake Erie to Lake Ontario (he thought improvements to shipping on the St. Lawrence River had more priority); the need for free and independent juries; elections to the Legislative Assembly; the difficulties that Americans had in receiving land grants in Upper Canada; and the disposition of public land through the private Canada Company. There was often the light (or heavy) touch of satire: on one occasion he wrote that wherever one turned, an individual with the likeness of the powerful William Allan was there, holding every

office imaginable. On another occasion he reported the
imaginary dream of one "Phil. Fudge": "Methought the
present Lieut. Governor had been superceded [sic] by
that mild and amiable person, [the fictitious] Lieutenant
Governor Sir Hudson Lowe." After the Reform lawyer
Marshall Bidwell was elected to the Legislative Assembly
in 1824, Mackenzie wrote: "It is said that when the news
of the election of young Bidwell reached little York, the
Attorney General was at dinner; he immediately took to
bed (leaving his dinner unfinished) and fasted three days.
The first day he spoke of leaving the law, to study divinity
under Dr Strachan, of course." (Strachan was the staunch
rector of St. James' Anglican Cathedral and a supporter of
the town's elite.) The paper published sermons and
reported on new buildings being constructed, the date the
Toronto bay was free of ice, marriages, deaths, the price
of commodities.

In April 1825 Mackenzie published his report on his
travels around Upper Canada, apparently mimicking
William Cobbett's report on the social conditions of
England, *Rural Rides*. It is much more than a travelogue,
noting the economic conditions of many centres including
Belleville, York, Niagara, and Kingston, citing the need
for better roads ("Truly the roads are the worst feature of
the country, and it takes a long time for a European to rec-
oncile himself to them"), and arguing that less support be
provided to British officials. In general the report is
breezy and chatty, the criticism muted and fairly offered.

But most of all, the *Advocate* dealt with politics. When

the Legislative Assembly was in session (usually the first two or three months of every year), the paper was published twice weekly in order to cover the debates thoroughly. The rest of the year it was generally published weekly. What's clear is Mackenzie's ability to write frequently and well about political matters. He labelled the May 4, 1826, issue "the latest and loudest blast of the Colonial Advocate sounded in the ears of the people of Upper Canada," saying, "Certain it is that the present Lt. Governor of Upper Canada is at present so justly unpopular that if we except the few who immediately depend on him for subsidence, there is scarcely a man in the colony but would be glad to learn he had taken his voyage down the St. Lawrence." He continued, "During the whole of our brief editorial campaign we have exercised with boldness the valuable privilege of thinking for ourselves; it may be here remarked that this boldness does not always attend the public exhibition of our countrymen; who are justly formed over the whole world for the more valuable quality of discretion."

From the beginning there was no question of Mackenzie's intent or impact. Within a month of the *Advocate*'s first issue, the editor of the *Upper Canada Gazette*, one of those "kept" papers Mackenzie complained of, denounced it as "a most insolent and wretched specimen of the total abandonment of all truth, principle, sense and decorum."

The newspaper was the foundation of his political life: it would give people information so they could form their own opinions. He trusted the ability of ordinary people to come to reasonable conclusions if they had the relevant information and the opportunity to discuss the issue. "The difference between passive obedience and non-resistance to a tyrannical government," he wrote in an early issue of the *Advocate*, "as compared with free discussion of the public measures of a represented and responsible one, is known by our meanest peasants." His newspapers (the *Colonial Advocate* was succeeded by several others over the next thirty-five years) served that purpose in extraordinary ways, aided by his ability to use rhetoric to seal an argument. Perhaps the best example of effective invective was his definition of the ruling families as the "Family Compact," a name that still survives in Ontario to describe a ruling clique. Mackenzie named the members of Upper Canada's Family Compact, showed how they were related, and described the way they wielded power.

Where the term "family compact" came from is not entirely settled. Thomas Dalton published a pamphlet in 1824 in Kingston referring to the elite of that city as "all one family compacted junto." In a letter written in 1828, Marshall Bidwell referred to the "measures to be adopted to relieve this province from the evils which a family compact have brought upon it." The words didn't see further use for another five years, when Mackenzie popularized the phrase. It's entirely possible the two usages are unrelated.

The Family Compact played a large role in the public life of Upper Canada and of its government, which consisted of three parts. The Legislative Assembly was an elected body with a broad franchise that included virtually all men who owned property and some who rented. This franchise was much more inclusive than that in Britain at the time.

The Legislative Council was an appointed body serving somewhat as a House of Lords. Its members were appointed for life by the lieutenant-governor (himself appointed by the English government). The council was not responsible to the assembly, yet decisions of the assembly needed its ratification to become effective, and it could veto decisions it didn't like. The council used that power with great frequency, robbing the popularly elected assembly of any real power. Sometimes the council refused to follow the advice of the lieutenant-governor.

The third organ of government was the Executive Council, whose members were appointed by and responsible to the lieutenant-governor during the term of their appointment. The governor and his advisers were in control of all decisions. The assembly might have been the most responsive and responsible arm of government, but it was the least powerful.

The imbalance of power was further sullied, according to Mackenzie, by a small group of people who held the key positions in these government structures, forming a Family Compact in control of decision-making in Upper Canada. Its members controlled the Legislative and Executive Councils, and some occupied a number of positions. For instance, John Strachan, the leading voice of the Anglican Church, was appointed to both the Executive Council and the Legislative Council.

Members of the Family Compact specialized "in profiteering through government office." Their alliance with the Compact often resulted in appointment to lucrative government positions such as sheriff, postmaster, or judge. Worse than that patronage, in Mackenzie's eyes, was that they operated as an aristocracy which assumed it knew best and could make the best decisions for the ordinary people of the province.

The popularly elected assembly would never have the power it required, Mackenzie thought, "unless the means of bribery and corruption be taken out of the hands of the vindictive family faction, and the people be granted the constitutional control over the public revenue and property which is so essential to good government." His fellow reformer Robert Baldwin put it slightly differently: Canada needed "responsible government," in which the key elements of government institutions were responsible to the electorate. Mackenzie rarely used the term.

"This family connection rules Upper Canada," Mackenzie wrote in the *Colonial Advocate*, "a dozen of nobodies and a few placemen, pensioners and individuals of well-known narrow and bigoted principles; the whole of the revenues of Upper Canada are in reality at their mercy; they are paymasters, receivers, auditors, King, Lords, and Commons!" On his return from England in 1833, Mackenzie published the names of those he saw as members of the Family Compact, along with their family linkages, their government positions, and (when known) their annual income from government. His description is an amazingly succinct model for describing a power structure. The first named, D'Arcy Boulton, is followed by his four sons; then follow brothers-in-law, more in-laws, sons, nephews, and cousins. Every man on the list was related by blood or marriage to at least one other.

These individuals held the cream of the appointed positions in Upper Canada. They were judges, sheriffs, postmasters, members of the Legislative Council, and bank directors. Their incomes, at a time when a hundred pounds a year provided a very comfortable life for a family, were substantial.

Mackenzie's description is simple and to the point:

A Political Union

The following curious but accurate statement will convey to the minds of liberal Englishmen, a tolerably fair picture of colonial rule. When I left Upper Canada last year some of the offices, sinecures, and pensions of the government were divided as follows:

1. D'Arcy Boulton, senior, a retired pensioner, £500, sterling.
2. Henry, son to No. 1, Attorney-General and Bank Solicitor, £2400.
3. D'Arcy, son to No. 1, Auditor-General, Master in Chancery, Police Justice, &c. Income unknown.
4. William, son to No. 1, Church Missionary, King's College Professor, &c., £650.

5. George, son to No. 1, Registrar of Northumberland, Member of Assembly for Durham, &c. Income unknown.

6. John Beverly [sic] Robinson, brother-in-law to No. 3, Chief Justice of Upper Canada, Member for life of the Legislative Council, Speaker of ditto, £2000.

7. Peter, brother of No. 6, Member of the Executive Council, Member for life of the Legislative Council, Crown Land Commissioner, Surveyor General of Woods, Clergy Reserve Commissioner, &c. £1399.

8. William, brother to Nos. 6 & 7, Postmaster of Newmarket, Member of Assembly for Simcoe, Government Contractor, Colonel of Militia, Justice of the Peace, &c. Income unknown.

9. James Jones, brother-in-law to No. 2, Judge of the District Court in three districts containing eight counties, and filling a number of other offices. Income about £1000.

10. Charles, brother to No. 9, Member for life of Legislative Council. Justice of the Peace in twenty-seven counties, &c.

11. Alpheus, brother to Nos. 9 and 10, Collector of Customs, Prescott, Postmaster at ditto, Agent for Government Bank at ditto, &c. income £100.

12. Levius P. Sherwood, brother-in-law to Nos. 9, 10, 11, one of the Justices of the Court of King's Bench. Income £1000.

13. Henry, son to No. 12, Clerk of Assize, &c.
14. John Elmsley, son-in-law to No. 12, Member of the Legislative Council for life, Bank Director, Justice of the Peace, &c.
15. Charles Heward, nephew to No. 6, Clerk of the District Court &c, Income £400.
16. James B. Macaulay, brother-in-law to Nos. 17 and 19. One of the Justices of the Court of King's Bench. Income £1000.
17. Christopher Alexander Hagerman, brother-in-law to No. 16, Solicitor-General, £800.
18. John M'Gill, a relation of Nos. 16 and 17. Legislative Councillor for life. Pensioner. £500.
19. & 20. W. Allan and George Crookshanks, connections by marriage of 16 and 17, Legislative Councillors for life, the latter President of the Bank. £500.
20. (as above)
21. Henry James, cousin to Nos. 9, 10 &c. Postmaster of Brockville, Justice of the Peace, Member of the Assembly for Brockville. Income unknown.
22. Wm. Dummer Powell, father of No. 24, Legislative Councillor for life. Justice of the Peace, Pensioner. Pension £1000.
23. Samuel Peters Jarvis, son-in-law of No. 22, Clerk of the Crown in Chancery, Deputy Secretary of the Province, Bank Director, &c. Income unknown.

24. Grant, son of No. 22, Clerk of the Legislative
    Council, Police Justice, Judge Home District
    Court, Official Principal of Probate Court,
    Commissioner of Customs, &c, Income. £675.
25. William M., cousin to No. 23, High Sheriff, Gore
    District, Member of Assembly. Income £900.
26. William B. cousin to Nos. 23 and 25, High Sheriff,
    Home District, Member of Assembly. Income
    £900.
27. Adiel Sherwood, cousin to No. 12. High Sheriff of
    Johnstown, and Treasurer of that district. Income
    from £500 to £800.
28. George Sherwood, son to No. 12, Clerk of Assize.
29. John Strachan, their family tutor and politician
    schoolmaster, archdeacon and rector of York,
    Member of the Executive and Legislative
    Councils, President of the University, President of
    the Board of Education, and twenty other situa-
    tions. Income, on an average of years, upwards of
    £1800.
30. Thomas Mercer Jones, son-in-law to No. 29,
    associated with No. 19, as the Canada Company's
    agents and managers in Canada.

Many of the names on Mackenzie's index are familiar
to Torontonians more than a century and a half later since
they grace the city's streets: Strachan Avenue, Boulton
Street, Sherwood Avenue, Jarvis Street, McGill Street,
Hagerman Street. (Macaulay Street was gobbled up by

the downtown Eaton Centre in the early 1970s.) In contrast, the names of prominent Reform leaders such as Samuel Lount and Peter Matthews, two patriots hanged for their parts in the Rebellion of 1837, have faded from memory, achieving none of the respectability offered through a street name.

Mackenzie took to calling the Family Compact the "thirty tyrants" for the way they exercised power. In full and delightful flight, he wrote:

> The "thirty tyrants" proceed in their systematic efforts to destroy good legislative measures; I may as well add in this place, that besides the salaries of its officers fixed by law, and the places and pensions and salaries and other things, your property, which its members unjustly enjoy, the legislative council demanded out of the public chest last winter, for silk curtains, velvet for their throne, tassels, hangings, Turkey carpeting, chairs of state, perfumery, gilding for a crown to their throne, presents to their servants, douceurs to some of themselves, and decorations for their chambers, a sum of money equal to about twelve thousand dollars, and got it too without a murmur or even an enquiry, three out of every four of your sapient representatives sanctioning the act of plunder, of robbery I might say, but I like to use mild expressions.

Personal enhancement at public expense is an entertaining folly when described by Mackenzie, and it continues to be a common political temptation. But for Mackenzie it was a sign of the larger evil, namely that the Family Compact assumed it knew best and, knowing that, saw no need or desire to share information or decision-making. It was his belief that legislators had a duty to educate people about public affairs so they could participate in them. The Family Compact rejected that approach, preferring to maintain ignorance in order to exercise control. "How can those who do their utmost to prevent the English people from being educated," he wrote, "in order that an Aristocracy may be necessary to control them, desire for us that moral, religious and educated population which would render the existence of an aristocracy in the government unnecessary? One thing is certain — no free popular government can exist unless the people are informed."

In late 1824, six months after the *Colonial Advocate* was established, Mackenzie moved his publishing business and his growing family — he and Isabel now had an infant daughter named after her mother — back to York. The town now had sixteen hundred residents and 2,887 private buildings — double the number of 1816 — of which 48 were shops. Mackenzie found a home for his family and his printing business in a building at the corner of Frederick Street and Palace (now Front) Street in the centre of town, equidistant from the new Bank of Upper Canada on Duchess (now Adelaide) Street and the market at Front and New (now Jarvis) Street. Mr. Justice William Campbell's red brick Georgian house sat at the head of Frederick Street (it has since been moved to the northwest corner of University and Queen Streets), and the Toronto harbour was at the south end.

The Legislative Assembly's chambers, located near Palace Street and Berkeley Street, had been rebuilt in 1819 after being burned by the invading Americans half a dozen years earlier, and it burned down again just months after Mackenzie moved to York. The assembly sought temporary meeting space in the hospital which had been built on the west side of the town, and Mackenzie used the occasion to comment that "the senators shall be thoroughly physicked, blistered, bled, purged, scorned, and cleansed from all their corruptions, diseases, impunities, and evil propensities...[and] you will find, then, that they will recover strength to vote large salaries to people who don't deserve them, strength enough to impose new imposts upon the peasantry, who trust in them."

The relocation to York had been traumatic. Isabel was nineteen months old when the move took place. She caught smallpox on the voyage from Queenston and died a few days before Christmas. It was the second recent death in the family — an unnamed baby daughter had died in Queenston on September 1. Mackenzie was dearly moved by the death, and issued a public declaration that no other member of the family suffered from smallpox.

The newspaper business did not flourish financially, but it was widely influential for the reform cause. Forty-three issues of the *Advocate* were published in the first twelve months, and in January 1825 the circulation was

listed as 830 copies. Mackenzie published news that
people wanted to read as well as strong opinion about the
manner in which he felt Upper Canada was being governed. But the illustrious readers in Britain, France, other
British colonies, the United States, and Upper Canada
continued to incur postal costs without returning subscription revenue. By mid-1825 Mackenzie was in enough debt
to cease publication for six months, but he found enough
money to start up again. This became a pattern, as debts
ebbed and flowed.

In an early issue of the *Advocate*, Mackenzie complained that paper manufactured in the United States
came into Upper Canada duty-free. He thought that if a
paper mill were be established in the province, the economy would benefit considerably. He organized a meeting
in York in 1825 and prepared a petition asking the
Legislative Assembly to support the cause. In 1826 the
assembly offered a reward of 125 pounds to the first
paper mill in Upper Canada. As a result of this challenge,
a mill was established in Flamborough, near Dundas; and
a few months later, in August 1827, a second mill was
established on the Don River, at what was then called Don
Mills (now Todmorden Mills), where the town's first
sawmill had been built in 1795 to saw the lumber for John
Graves Simcoe's cottage, Castle Frank. Mackenzie purchased paper from both mills, finally settling on the more
local product because of the political sympathies of the
owners, although he complained about the paper's quality.

In May 1826, Mackenzie hinted in his paper that he

would retire, and a new editor would be appointed. This appeared to be a ruse to create an illusionary distance between himself and the person he claimed would be the new editor. According to the fictitious commentary he provided of meetings held to select a new editor, the person chosen was one Patrick Swift, said to be "a grand nephew of the famous Doctor Jonathan Swift," author of the satire *Gulliver's Travels.* The issues of May 18 and May 25 contained satirical commentaries about affairs in Upper Canada, reported as the transcript of conversations between Patrick Swift and his colleagues.

The commentaries touched on people and events then generally known in Upper Canada, and were spiced with denunciations and strong opinions. There were numerous scurrilous comments on members of the Family Compact. James Macaulay was referred to as that "pitiful mean-looking parasite Macaulay"; John Strachan, "a little awk-ward looking body with a crooked shovel hat"; William Allan, a "boot polisher." On occasion the comments were downright nasty. Mackenzie made a strong jibe at the wife of the lieutenant-governor, Sir Peregrine Maitland. Mackenzie implied that Lady Sarah was a "base born descendant" and had eloped with Sir Peregrine, who was nothing more than a "low born fortune hunter." Seizing on a theme to which he would return on many other occasions, Swift said Lady Sarah came from "a family who have for centuries been a dead weight on the people of London and are now likely to become a heavier burden on those of Upper Canada." That, along with many other swipes at the leaders of the government, did not endear the *Colonial Advocate* to members of the Family Compact. One of the hazards of confronting powerful and influential forces in society is that they will not sit idly by, but will hit back. These issues of the paper proved to be the breaking point.

Just after six o'clock on the evening of June 8, 1826, a number of young men broke into Mackenzie's house, where his printing press was located. Mackenzie was not at home, although his seventy-five-year-old mother and young son were upstairs during the break-in. The gang stole the type and hurled it into the bay at the end of the street. Benignly watching the action from across the street and taking no steps to intervene were the magistrate William Allan and a clerk of the peace, Stephen Heward.

The perpetrators were the young sons of the Family Compact and their friends, including John Lyons, Samuel Jarvis, Peter McDougall, Henry Sherwood, Charles Baby, Raymond Baby, Charles Heward (Stephen's son), James King, and Charles Richardson. Seven of the gang were either lawyers or law students. This group's mission was to destroy the device which Mackenzie had used so effectively, his newspaper.

The historian Chris Raible calls the episode the "Types Riot." He thinks there is reasonable evidence to believe that the incident might have been provoked by John Lyons, clerk of the lieutenant governor, who knew the distress caused to Lady Sarah by the insinuations made by Mackenzie. Lyons was the person around whom the

Family Compact rallied to go after Mackenzie, although a few years later, perhaps as a cover-up, Samuel Jarvis shouldered blame as the ringleader and claimed it was just the prank of a few young men.

As it turned out, it was a very foolish prank. Mackenzie sought restitution in court. The judge with carriage of the case was William Campbell, a certified member of the Family Compact by virtue of his position. But Campbell was also a man of principle. He had rebuffed pressure to behave improperly as attorney general of Nova Scotia two decades earlier, and for that was removed from his position. He appealed to English authorities, who were clearly impressed with his honesty, appointing him a judge in Upper Canada in 1811.

His friendships did not cloud his principles in this case. Mackenzie rejected a settlement offer of 200 pounds, expecting his lawyer Marshall Bidwell to do better at trial. Campbell's rulings were considered fair, and Mackenzie obtained a jury decision which awarded him more than 650 pounds. He was able to pay off his debts and re-establish the newspaper. The Types Riot significantly benefitted Mackenzie.

Unfortunately, Mackenzie had a penchant for diverting people from his clear analysis and strong statements by taking foolish action. His strength was attacking government leaders for their refusal to govern in open and transparent ways, and demanding that people should be educated on public issues. His diversion on this occasion was the reckless insulting of the lieutenant-governor's wife, and his serious criticism of government was lost in the fireworks. It seems that this characteristic (some would elevate it to a character flaw) has probably led to the many conflicting opinions about his actions.

The *Colonial Advocate*'s barrage against the Family Compact continued. Within two years Mackenzie was elected to the Legislative Assembly, where he would pursue his work in informing the people from a new vantage point.

4 · Mackenzie Enters the Assembly

MACKENZIE RAN FOR a seat in the Legislative Assembly in 1828. He was certainly not the first outspoken voice of reform to seek and secure elected office in Upper Canada, but prior to the publication of the *Colonial Advocate*, their numbers were few. Perhaps the financial and career benefits of siding with the lieutenant-governor and his supporters discouraged opposition. Perhaps the idea of placing public decision-making in the control of ordinary people was too new to attract consistent support. In any case, the legacies of Mackenzie's few reform-minded predecessors are not all that clear or consistent.

There seem to have been only three strong opposition

politicians of note in Upper Canada before Mackenzie. Robert Thorpe, born in Ireland in 1773, arrived in Upper Canada in 1805 fresh from a four-year appointment as chief justice of Prince Edward Island. He was an early advocate of the view that the Legislative Council, the main body advising the lieutenant-governor, should be responsible to the elected Assembly rather than to the lieutenant-governor. (This view formed the basis of "responsible government," which was finally established in the late 1840s.) Thorpe also thought the elected assembly, not the Executive Council, should control revenues.

As a judge, Thorpe looked for ways that ordinary people could speak up and comment on the government they lived under in Upper Canada, and he found a good device: he asked grand juries to voice their grievances on such matters. He was thought to have been the author of a pamphlet on these questions. Thorpe was elected to the assembly in 1806, replacing another progressive, the lawyer William Weekes, who had been killed in a duel. In 1807, when it seemed clear he would lose his only source of income, his judgeship — presumably because of his reforming agenda — he left the country. He was later appointed a judge in Sierra Leone.

Joseph Willcocks came to Upper Canada in 1799 and gained a position as sheriff, which was taken away when he publicly supported Thorpe. He was elected to the Assembly in 1808 in a Niagara riding. His agenda was broader than Thorpe's, but didn't include such a focus on responsible government. He advocated electoral reform,

reform of juries, reduced public salaries, and government appointments by the assembly, not by the lieutenant-governor. He opposed the dominance of the Church of England, which was so strong that for a brief period elected members of the Methodist persuasion were not permitted to sit in the assembly. Willcocks served in the assembly until 1813. He was so discouraged by the assembly's loss of power to the lieutenant-governor because of the pressures exerted by the war against American aggression in 1812 that he offered his services to the Americans. He was wounded fighting for the American side and died in September 1814.

The third clear voice of reform before Mackenzie was Robert Gourlay. Like Mackenzie, Gourlay was born in Scotland, in 1778. His concern was bettering the plight of the rural poor, and as part of his training in agricultural science, he learned to gather information through surveys of public opinion. He came to Upper Canada in 1817 for reasons that are not entirely clear, and turned his attention to encouraging more immigration, perhaps to provide a more ready market for a nine-hundred-acre parcel of land in the Niagara area which his wife had inherited. To build a base of support for more immigration, he conducted a statistical survey using a long questionnaire. One question asked of Upper Canadians was what "retards the improvement of your township in particular, or the province in general, and what would most contribute to the same?"

For the government, this was a touchy subject. There was much discontent following the War of 1812. Those

who had suffered from the American invasion had not
been compensated for their losses, nor had militia been
given the land they had been promised. By order of the
lieutenant-governor, land sales to Americans had been
frozen, and Americans were not permitted to immigrate
to Upper Canada. Government leaders were not pleased
with opening debate about problems facing Upper Canada, but Gourlay pressed on. In 1818, he openly challenged the government on the restriction against selling to
Americans and the ban on American immigration. His
writing was vitriolic: "The Constitution of the province is
in danger, all the blessings of the social compact are running to waste," and "it is the system that blasts every hope
of good; and till the system is overturned, it is vain to
expect anything of value from change of representatives
or governors."

Gourlay raised the heat by holding public meetings
throughout Upper Canada in May and June 1818 where
these issues, as well as the control of patronage and the
reform of the tax system, were fully debated. He was one
of the first people in Upper Canada to make good use of
township meetings as a forum for debate and discussion
on large public issues, a practice Radicals such as Henry
Hunt and George Kinloch had used in Britain to good
effect, and one that Mackenzie relied on throughout his
political career to great advantage. One historian says
Gourlay was "the first great agitator, demagogue and
organizer, who taught the people how to make their power
felt." Gourlay often concluded meetings with the adoption

of resolutions. Attorney General John Beverley Robinson looked hard for some legal justification to suppress such meetings but concluded "that neither the township meetings, nor the convention that is to assemble at York can be prevented, or opposed by any constitutional exercise of authority." Yet the government wished to take action, and Gourlay was charged with seditious libel. While on bail, he again tested the establishment by holding the promised convention in York. In mid-August 1818 the trial was held, and the jury gave legitimacy to Gourlay's actions by issuing a verdict of not guilty.

Gourlay continued his meetings, which Robinson said "seem to me to be dangerous in this country, chiefly from their example, as they point out the mode by which popular movements on pretences less specious than the present, can be effected." The government would not let the matter rest. In October 1818 a bill was introduced to prevent such meetings. It banned meetings "under pretence of deliberating upon matters of public concern or of preparing or presenting petitions, complaints, remonstrances and declarations and other addresses to the King, or to both or to either Houses of Parliament for alteration of matters established by law, or redress of alleged grievances in Church and State." Its authors feared meetings might "be made use of by factious and seditious persons to the violation of the public peace, and manifest encouragement of riot, tumult, and disorder."

Many public meetings were held in protest, but the bill became law on November 27, 1818. On December 3

Gourlay published an article against the legislation in the *Niagara Spectator* entitled "Gagg'd-gagg'd, by Jingo," and he urged that more public meetings be called. On December 21, he was charged and ordered to leave the province by January 1, 1819. He did not leave. On January 4, he was arrested and put in jail, although his letters continued to be published in the *Niagara Spectator*. The publisher was later convicted of sedition and the *Spectator* folded. Gourlay was kept in jail until his trial in August, when he was found guilty and immediately expelled.

A few months after Gourlay's expulsion, four of his supporters were elected in the Niagara peninsula: John Clark, William J. Kerr, Robert Hamilton, and Robert Randall. Gourlay was obviously speaking for more than just himself. In 1821 Robert Nichol was elected, advocating elected control of provincial revenues, one of Gourlay's causes.

Mackenzie, who arrived in Upper Canada a year after Gourlay was ousted, often referred to what had happened to Gourlay for voicing public concerns, and treated it as a black mark against the Family Compact. He didn't let his readers forget these events, and he gave them a significant place in the Patrick Swift commentaries in the *Colonial Advocate*. Attorney General Robinson made a link between the two men early in Mackenzie's career, saying "another reptile of the Gourlay species has sprung up in a Mr. William Mackenzie of Dundas ... a conceited red-headed fellow with an apron. ... He said that I am the most subtle advocate of arbitrary power ... what vermin!"

Clearly Gourlay made a strong impact and did the early work in beginning to define a Reform agenda for Upper Canada. Like Mackenzie, he is not universally admired. One historian says of Gourlay "Beyond providing the useful myth of this martyrdom at the hands of a reactionary oligarchy, and perhaps some useful organizational techniques, he seems temporarily to have short-circuited reform. His egotism obscured its aims, his style brought it disrepute, and his petitioning technique was a tactical blind alley." Others take an even harsher view.

This was the ground upon which Mackenzie began his career as a Reform politician: the mere handful of opposition voices that had concentrated on larger public problems in Upper Canada. There was no "democratic" agenda for him to adopt. At best there was a rather loose set of complaints known to generate some popular support. Others shared this Reform political ground, and some were already members of the assembly. Marshall Bidwell, for one, was elected to the Assembly in 1825, and was fully apprised of the difficulties of Americans owning land since his father, Barnabas Bidwell, a supporter of Gourlay, was elected to the assembly in 1821 but then expelled as an "alien" since he had been born in United States. Another was the successful tanner Jesse Ketchum. Other reform-minded members of the assembly in 1825 were Peter Perry, John Rolph, and Captain John Matthews, whose common cause was their opposition to the Church of England as an established church. William Baldwin, father of Robert Baldwin, was another voice of reform and had been elected earlier, although he was not a member of the assembly at this time. None had the radical streak that Mackenzie had been immersed in back in the old country; they were generally urbane or intellectual in their approaches.

Early in 1827 Mackenzie became involved in pressing for the rights of Americans in Canada. A committee was established with Mackenzie as its secretary, and it met in his home. The issue was the Alien Question. Family Compact members, fearing American democratic influences following the War of 1812, convinced the lieutenant-governor, Francis Gore, to require that those swearing loyalty to the Crown could be naturalized citizens (and thus allowed to own land) after seven years' residency. It was a sweeping change, since it implied that the United Empire Loyalists who had come to Upper Canada in 1783 were not citizens — and thus could not own land. Yet it was often the promise of ownership which led to the improvement of land, and an inability to own land was a major stumbling block to immigration and economic development, as Gourlay had already made clear. Robert Nichol, a member of the assembly, introduced a motion in early 1817 to rectify the situation, but Lieutenant-Governor Gore was so worried it would carry that he prorogued the assembly. This was one factor that set Gourlay in motion.

Neither the British government nor the Upper Canada government was willing to take responsibility for settling the issue. It was tossed back and forth like a hot potato. In

1824 a court ruled that residents of United States in 1783 could not be British citizens. This and other events provoked the creation of the committee. Jesse Ketchum, a successful and progressive businessman, was active in the committee, as was William Baldwin. The colonial authorities agreed to change the situation, and the Legislative Council proposed a bill that went only part way toward resolving the problem. Ketchum, Bidwell, and Baldwin all played a large part in raising public opinion against the Legislative Council's Alien Bill in 1827. It required United Empire Loyalists who had emigrated from the United States to retake the oath of allegiance and reregister with authorities. It was a contentious issue that Mackenzie reported on in the *Advocate*.

A petition was circulated advocating complete redress, and some fifteen thousand people signed it. The petition was then taken by Mackenzie's friend, Robert Randall, to Britain and presented to the English government, where support was found. When Marshall Bidwell introduced a bill in the assembly allowing anyone to own land, it passed the assembly as the Naturalization Act and was supported — rather than disallowed — by the Legislative Council. It was an early lesson for Mackenzie in the power of direct appeal to London.

The other significant issue of the time was the dismissal of Judge John Willis. Willis argued that the court could not sit in the absence of the chief judge, then ill in England, and his refusal to sit delayed certain important trials. His dismissal was the subject of a number of large public meetings during the summer of 1828, again reported by Mackenzie.

But Mackenzie did not consult any of the leaders of the protests about whether he should be a candidate: he decided on his own to run for elected office. Since he had begun publishing the *Colonial Advocate*, Mackenzie had been publicly struggling to define the role and the responsibilities of the elected representative. It was a new kind of problem, since the notion of public decision-makers representing people other than themselves was so recent an idea, just being experimented with in Canada. In the United States, Thomas Jefferson had urged the cause of democracy and government of, by, and for the people, but even there progress was made slowly. For instance, the strongest advocate of the common man, Andrew Jackson, was not elected president until 1828. Mackenzie did not have many role models when thinking about these issues. Yet he had high expectations of the character of those elected to public office as representatives. In the first issue of the *Colonial Advocate*, he defined the task in this way: "We very much want men in Canada, who have received a liberal education; men untainted by the enjoyment of power and place, who, if called on, would not hesitate to sacrifice their personal interests for the good of their country; and who, if elected to our house of assembly, would return to their homes at the end of a fourth or fifth session, as free from the enthralments of patronage and place, of honours and pensions, as when they were first placed in the honourable situation of guardians of their country's rights."

A year later, he again returned to the subject, in a more verbose way. Mackenzie did not see the elected representative acting in a vacuum, but ascribed an educative function to that person so that those represented would be informed and have opinions of their own, which they would pass along to those elected to office. There is nothing passive about his idea of how representation should work. He saw it as interactive, with information and opinions flowing back and forth in the community and between the community and the elected members. The opinions he valued are those not of the rabble but of the informed citizen.

A Patriot is none of your raving, railing, ranting, enquiring, accusing radicals — nor is he one of your idle, stall-fed, greasy, good for nothing sinecurists or pluralists — he is in deed and in truth a friend to his country. He studies the laws and institutions of his nation, that he may improve others, endeavours rather to cultivate the acquaintance of, and shew a correct example to the better informed Classes; he associates only with those whose private conduct is in unison with their public professions. Is not a mob hunter, nor a lecturer of the multitude; desires rather the secret approbation of the enlightened few than the ephemeral popularity of the many.

If he is a member of Parliament he looks carefully into the merits of the question and votes consistently with his conscience, whether with or against the ministry. He is neither a place hunter, nor a sinecure hunter. He promises his constituents very little, but tries to perform a great deal. Finally he is among the last of men who would countenance political "gamblers and blacklegs"; but a wise, manly and vigilant administration is his delight. — Is there one among your ranks who answers to this description? Let him come forward. He alone can save you from confusion and defeat.

Mackenzie placed much emphasis on the representative's task of creating an informed populace. Perhaps this focus emerged from his life as a journalist, perhaps from his conception of good government: in any case he spent a great deal of time and energy ensuring that the public was as fully informed as possible. His writings as an elected person are replete with descriptions of how he provided relevant written documents and participated in public gatherings for the purpose of sharing information and helping to form intelligent public opinions. His criticisms of other newspapers often came down to the fact that they did not encourage this kind of debate and did not provide the necessary information to help citizens in this task. At the same time, he was not a populist, willing to feed back to the public what it wanted to hear. While he did not hesitate in giving voice to his own opinions, he saw the more important role as giving others the information necessary for them to come to their own conclusions.

These are the values with which Mackenzie entered the arena of the elected representative. He declared his intention to run in an open letter in December 1827, well before the election actually occurred in July 1828.

To the electors of the County of York

Gentlemen: — I have the honour to inform you that it is my intention to come forward at the next Election of Members to serve for your County in the Provincial Parliament and I most respectfully solicit your votes and support.

I have no end in view but the well being of the people at large — no ambition to serve, but that of contributing to the happiness and prosperity of our common country. The influence and authority with which you may invest me, shall always be directed, according to the best of my judgment, for the general good; and it will be my care to uphold your rights to the utmost of my power, with that firmness, moderation, and *perseverance,* which becomes the representative of a free people.

I have ever been opposed to ecclesiastical domination; it is at enmity with the free spirit of Christianity: and nations which have bowed to its yoke, are become the dark abodes of ignorance and superstition — oppression and misery.

That corrupt, powerful and long-endured influence which has hitherto interfered with your rights and liberties, can only be overthrown by your unanimity and zeal. An independent House of Assembly, to Upper

Canada, would be inestimable.

I have been a careful observer of the conduct of the people's representatives in the colonial assemblies: I have seen men in whom was placed the utmost confidence, fall from their integrity and betray their sacred trust — men too, who had entered upon their legislative duties with the best intentions towards the people, and who evinced for a time a firm determination to support their rights. But there are others who continue to maintain and uphold the interests of their country, unshaken and undismayed; who consider it their highest honour to persevere in a faithful discharge of their public duties, and eagerly strive to deserve the good will, the affection, and the confidence of their fellow subjects.

Among this latter class I am desirous of being numbered; and unless I shall be found deserting the cause of the people, I trust that the people will never desert me.

Accept my sincere thanks for the abundant proofs of kindness and confidence, and for the liberal assurances of support, with which you have honoured me, and believe me,

Gentlemen, Your faithful humble servant,

W. L. Mackenzie.

York, 17th December 1827.

The letter was followed by his attendance at a large political meeting in Markham, just north of Toronto, in January 1828. There Mackenzie proposed a long series of motions touching on the issues of the day: disposal of the

Clergy Reserves; opposition to an established state religion in Upper Canada; establishment of a university; more
power for the assembly; a less costly civil court system;
improvement of the St. Lawrence River system rather than
construction of the Welland Canal; and removing judges
from politics. It was the familiar list of issues that received
much space in the *Colonial Advocate*. After those motions
were approved, Mackenzie reported, "The chairman
needed a resolution which had been duly seconded, nomi-
nating and recommending Mr. William Lyon Mackenzie,
of York, as a fit and proper person to represent the County
at the next general election. The question was put, the
freeholders divided, and a very large majority were found
to be in favour of the resolution which carried accordingly."

Since the riding elected two representatives, the
meeting went on to also nominate the businessman and
Reformer Jesse Ketchum. A further candidate, William
Roe, was also endorsed by the meeting, although the
nomination of James Small, who had been one of
Mackenzie's lawyers on the Types Riot case, was left
undecided. Mackenzie had started his political career in
Upper Canada true to his principles: give people information, help ensure there is a strong debate, then ask the
community to make a decision. Some writers portray
Mackenzie as a solitary figure making his way into politics, without consultation, but it is apparent that he relied
on public support to get underway. He may have argued
that he would be his own man, but only after receiving
public backing and encouragement.

In the February 14 issue of the *Advocate*, he published the appeal to voters that had been circulated in December, and on March 13 he reprinted his recent speech to the Constitutional Society of Upper Canada. From that time until the election, four months later, Mackenzie appeared to provide himself no special forum in the *Advocate*. The newspaper continued to simply play its familiar proactive role. Starting on May 22 and continuing weekly until early July, Mackenzie published a lengthy series of articles titled "The Parliament Black Book for Upper Canada, or Official Corruption and Hypocrisy Unmasked." It was a list of wrongdoings, starting from before Gourlay's time and continuing into the present. Each incident was numbered, and by July 2, he had reached 104. On July 19, the eve of the election, he included a modest and brief note: "My political principles are well known to most of you, and I shall only add, that on the day of the election I will be a candidate for your suffrages; and, if successful at the hustings, I trust that you will never have occasion, from my parliamentary conduct, to repent your choice."

There were four candidates in the election, as the Markham meeting had hinted. Ketchum received the most votes, and Mackenzie was elected a strong second. These results were not noted in the *Advocate*, perhaps because those elected were not sworn in and given official status until almost six months later.

The new assembly met on January 8, 1829. Since there were no political parties, it was unclear what direction the new Legislative Assembly would take — save that its most democratic impulses would in all likelihood be constrained by a Legislative Council consisting of Family Compact members appointed for life. The tenor of the assembly was made clear with its first decision: Marshall Bidwell was elected Speaker. John Rolph, a doctor who had been elected for the first time, then moved a motion of non-confidence in the government's advisers, and it carried by a vote of 37 to 1. The vast majority of the 48 members of the Assembly clearly consisted of people like Mackenzie who supported Reform positions; there was also a smattering of Tories who resented the power of the Family Compact. It was the first time the assembly was dominated by those opposed to the lieutenant-governor and his appointees.

But because of the power of the Legislative Council to disallow decisions of the assembly, the Reform majority had only the opportunity to investigate and discuss abuses, not to provide substantive new direction. Mackenzie was very active, chairing a number of committees, although since the assembly sat for only a few months, the committees were unable to do much in the way of creating political momentum. (This assembly met from January 8 to March 20, 1829, and from January 8 to March 6, 1830.) The committees brought some attention to an issue and sometimes generated useful information, but often they did little more than putting forward ideas for the real government — the friends of the lieutenant-governor — to review.

Mackenzie chaired a select committee looking into the postal service, which was administered and operated by the postmaster general in England. Mackenzie recommended that it be a local authority, and that its revenues — he and others complained of the high costs of mail, particularly compared with postal rates in the United States — be used to improve postal service in Upper Canada rather than to generate a surplus for general revenues in Britain. Local control of the postal service was not secured until 1851, following the union of Upper and Lower Canada.

He chaired a committee on privileges of the assembly, specifically inquiring into the appointment of election returning officers. This was a subject to which he returned on many occasions and which he considered at much greater length in 1835, when he chaired the Grievances Committee. The question of corrupt elections was not resolved by his first foray into their details.

A third committee looked at banking and currency. Mackenzie feared the power of banks and tried (unsuccessfully) to ensure that no further banks were chartered in Upper Canada. Another committee looked at the poor condition of roads, and a fifth considered the power and authority of the Church of England. Mackenzie worked hard and complained about the very long hours which engaged his skills and energy.

But the Reformers were not cohesive or strategic enough to create a strong and believable direction for their myriad activities. Further, their best ideas were stopped cold by the Legislative Council and the Executive Council. Between 1829 and 1837, some fifty-three bills

passed by the assembly were rejected by the Legislative
Council. "In general," remarks one historian who was no
friend of Mackenzie, "in regard to proposals tending to
alter the established political and social order [that is,the
Legislative and Executive Councils] conservatism was
extreme."

Lord Durham, who was retained after the 1837 rebel-
lions to report on the state of political affairs in Canada,
was even more scathing about the power of the Executive
Council.

> The real advisers of the governor have, in fact, been the
> executive council, and an institution more singularly
> calculated for preventing the responsibility of the acts
> of government resting on anybody can hardly be imag-
> ined. It is a body of which the constitution somewhat
> resembles that of the Privy Council; it is bound by a
> similar oath of secrecy; it discharges in the same man-
> ner anomalous judicial functions; and its "consent and
> advice" are required in some cases in which the obser-
> vance of that form has been through a requisite check
> on the exercise of particular prerogatives of the Crown.
> But in other respects it bears a greater resemblance to
> a cabinet, the governor being in the habit of taking its
> advice on most of the important questions of his policy.
> But, as there is no division into departments in the coun-
> cil, there is no individual responsibility, and no individ-
> ual superintendence. Each member of the council takes
> an equal part in all the business brought before it. The

power of removing members being very rarely exercised, the council is, in fact, for the most part, composed of persons placed in it long ago; and the governor is obliged either to take the advice of persons in whom he has no confidence, or to consult only a portion of the council. The secrecy of the proceedings adds to the irresponsibility of the body; and when the governor takes an important step, it is not known, or not authentically known, whether he has taken the advice of this council or not, what members he has consulted, or by the advice of which of the body he has been finally guided. The responsibility of the executive council has been constantly demanded by the Reformers of Upper Canada, and occasionally by those of the Lower Province. But it is really difficult to conceive how desirable responsibility could be attained, except by altering the working of this cumbrous machine, and placing the business of the various departments of government in the hands of competent public officers.

Being elected to the Legislative Assembly clearly did not result in Mackenzie gaining even a small portion of the power exercised by a member of the Family Compact. Further, the limited meeting periods of the assembly meant that it was unable to generate a consistent and sustained approach to issues. The Executive Council functioned twelve months a year.

Between the 1829 and 1830 sessions of the Assembly, Mackenzie travelled in the United States for several

months. Equality's great American proponent, Andrew
Jackson, had been elected president the year previous,
and Mackenzie met with him in Washington and became
an admirer in a mild fashion. He shared Jackson's values
about equality of opportunity but returned to Canada with
the thought that making the Canadian system work better
was wiser than introducing the American system. He
returned convinced that however desirable responsible
government might be, it was necessary to make the
Legislative Council elective, and to extend the same
system to all public officers. Of course, Mackenzie was
constrained by the understanding that praising American
practices often led to questions of loyalty, so he was careful in voicing his opinion of Jackson.

Two more children were born during these years:
Barbara, born in May 1827, who became mentally ill on
several occasions (it may have been manic depression)
and finally died a very sad, apparently self-inflicted death
in 1860; and Janet, born in April 1829, who married the
respected journalist Charles Lindsey in 1852. It is not
exactly clear where in York the family lived during this
period — perhaps on King Street near Toronto Street. It
appears the family left the house at Frederick and Palace
Streets during 1827.

On June 26, 1830, King George IV died, and since the
elected government was seen as an extension of the royal
person, the assembly was dissolved on September 10,
and a new election was called for late October. The
Reform bloom was about to be nipped in the bud.

5 · Mackenzie's Elections and Ejections

MACKENZIE PREPARED FOR the new election in 1830 by simplifying and clarifying the five issues most important to him, which he did with a succinct statement in the September 9 edition of the *Advocate*:

1. The entire control of the whole provincial revenues is required to be vested in the legislature — the territorial and hereditary revenues excepted.

2. The independence of the judges; or their removal to take place only upon a joint address of the two Houses, and their appointment from among men who have not embarked in the political business of the province.

3. A reform in the legislative council, which is now an assembly chiefly composed of persons wholly or partly dependent upon the executive government for their support.

4. An administration or executive government responsible to the province for its conduct.

5. Equal rights to each religious denomination, and an exclusion of every sect from a participation in temporal power.

He also gave renewed voice to his vision of the governing process. After serving in two sessions of the assembly, he confirmed the best process as one that was interactive and public in nature, not something that saw elected representatives acting on their own or in an isolated manner. Governing was a joint venture of representatives and the public: "An enlightened people are the only safe depository of the ultimate powers of society. The great object in the institutions of popular assemblies is that the people may be fully and freely represented; and in proportion as the structure of government gives influence to public opinion, it is essential that public opinion should be enlightened."

It was as though being an elected official had radicalized him, made him even more a man of the people. He reviewed the question of the need for a political party — the Reformers had been a ragged group at best, unable to act cohesively enough in the Assembly to create a strong and believable direction for their myriad activities — but came to a negative conclusion. He found political parties and factions abhorrent, not just because they made it more difficult for the representative to follow his conscience, but also because they placed a barrier in the way of experiencing a sense of community. "Mechanics of Upper Canada!" he warned. "Beware of secret associations — they are unfit for a free country! Beware of the spirit of party, of sects, and of factions; they are ever injurious to true liberty by dividing the people against each other."

Another barrier for Mackenzie was that he was the least ideological of public figures. He was opinionated about virtually everything, but he had the good grace to change according to knowledge and experience. Mackenzie hardly ever thought he had the definitive answer to anything — quite the reverse. He spent virtually his whole political career learning at first hand exactly what was going on and why.

Perhaps Mackenzie was careful to reiterate his policy beliefs and his political *modus operandi* at this time because he realized that he and his colleagues would not enjoy great success in the election, scheduled for the end of October. Two changes may have been apparent to Mackenzie, although neither found direct expression in the *Advocate*. First, the Reformers had kept the Assembly full of complaints and bravado for the past two years, but had not brought forward a believable enough program to widen Reform loyalties. Part of the problem was that real power lay with the Legislative and Executive Councils, so that as their proposals were constantly turned back by the councils, the Reformers appeared merely oppositional in nature, and not ready to rule. A Tory majority, in comparison, could pass legislation in the Assembly knowing that, even though there were differences between the Family Compact elite and elected Tories, it would probably receive a positive hearing and the necessary approvals from the councils, and thereby could give the Assembly the appearance of being a governing body. As well, Sir John Colborne was an attractive and amiable lieutenant-governor. He attracted sympathy and good will, and that spilled over to Tories running for a seat in the Assembly.

When the election came, Ketchum and Mackenzie were again returned for York County, the former with 616 votes, the latter with 570, considerably ahead of the other candidates, Simon Washburn and Richard Thorne. But Reformers in other ridings did poorly. Robert Baldwin was not re-elected. Nor was John Rolph, acknowledged leader of the Reformers in the Assembly for the past few terms. After this election the Assembly was controlled by the Tories, and they fully intended to make up for lost time.

When the Assembly began meeting on January 7, 1831, the Tory majority looked for some way to silence the "little manikin from York," as Attorney General Henry Boulton referred to him. Allan MacNab, a member of the Family Compact whom Mackenzie had successfully accused of breach of privilege in the previous session, levied a similar accusation against Mackenzie for distributing transcripts of Assembly debates. Mackenzie had the contract to publish Assembly debates and before the election had, at his own expense, distributed some 168 copies of them in ridings where he felt they might be effective in helping Reform candidates. Mackenzie believed "no more effective campaign document could be devised than a truthful record of the proceedings in the House." There was no accusation of inaccuracy, just that the Assembly had not authorized this distribution. MacNab's motion of censure against Mackenzie did not find majority support in the Assembly — the Tories themselves had done the same thing in the past, so even some Tories voted against the motion. But this signalled the kind of personal attack Mackenzie would face later in the year.

Mackenzie chaired a special committee which proposed that the growing towns in Upper Canada be given better representation. He proposed that voting be held on a single day, rather than on two or more days, and that voting be by secret ballot rather than by public declamation. These changes were not made until after the Rebellion of 1837.

For its part, the imperial government in London responded to a long-standing complaint of the Reformers. Reformers had vehemently opposed the colony's revenues being at the disposal of the lieutenant-governor and used for his priorities, and they had long advocated that the Assembly be given control over most revenues. The government now agreed and proposed, perhaps because the new majority favoured the Tory cause, to put some financial control in the hands of the Assembly. But there was a trade-off involved. In return for the Assembly achieving this power, the lieutenant-governor would gain unfettered control over government appointments and the salaries paid to them. Mackenzie howled, calling the legislation the Everlasting Salary Bill and denouncing it in the *Advocate*. But he and his colleagues were unable to find the votes to defeat it.

One issue Mackenzie concentrated on was elections, and how some areas of Upper Canada had more clout than others, since some constituencies were considerably smaller than others. This was not the British "rotten borough" problem that the great Reform Bill of 1832 would resolve. Rotten boroughs had representatives in Parliament but rarely had constituents. Here constituencies contained residents, but there were vast differences in the numbers served by a representative. Mackenzie described it as "inequality of representation," and stated, "I could name fifteen members in this House who have not altogether so many constituents as the honourable member for Lanark, my honourable colleague, and myself. I could show that twenty-six of the members of this House, being a majority of the whole, are returned by a population consisting of less than one third of the inhabitants of the province, while the other two-thirds are only permitted to send twenty-four members, or less than half the representation. Is it fair towards the freeholders that Hastings, Dundas, Haldimand, Niagara and Brockville should send hither seven members, each having one vote, while York County, with more than double the population of all these places taken together, sends only two members, each having but one vote?"

He noted that not everyone had the vote, but some were excluded by property qualification, and if that were put aside "the present system would be still more apparent." He cited his recent request that the assembly inquire into the operation of the Bank of Upper Canada, a motion that was defeated by a vote of 24 to 15, and stated: "On examination, I found that the 24 who were for hushing up enquiry represented a smaller number of the Canadian people than the 15 who voted in its favour." His complaints went unheeded.

By mid-March, the assembly had adjourned. Mackenzie travelled to Lower Canada to meet with reformers there, and his letters brim with the delight of the real world in all of its diversity and surprise. His trip took him to Quebec City and the following scene on a fair April morning:

One forenoon I went on board the ship *Airthy Castle*, from Bristol, immediately after her arrival. The passengers were in number 254, all in the hold or steerage; all English, from about Bristol, Bath, Frome, Warminster, Maiden Bradley, etc. I went below, and truly it was a curious sight. About 200 human beings, male and female, young, old and middle-aged; talking, singing, laughing, crying, eating, drinking, shaving, washing; some naked in bed, and others dressing to go ashore; handsome young women (perhaps some) and ugly old men, married and single, religious and irreligious. Here a grave matron chaunting selections from the last edition of the last new hymn book; there, a brawny plough-boy pouring forth the sweet melody of Robin Adair. These settlers were poor, but in general they were fine-looking people, and such as I was glad to see come to America. They had had a fine passage of about a month, and they told me that no more ship loads of settlers would come from the same quarter this year. I found that it was the intention of many of them to come to Upper Canada. Fortune may smile on some, and frown on others; but it is my opinion that few among them will forget being cooped up below deck for four weeks in a moveable bed-room, with 250 such fellow-lodgers as I have endeavoured to describe.

It would be hard to improve upon the delight, the early-summer optimism, or indeed on the first-hand experience of the immigration process. Mackenzie himself had come to Canada eleven years earlier, but there is nothing in this description aboard the *Airthy Castle* harkening back to that experience, no hint of contrast to his own state of affairs. His interest was in catching what was before his eyes and making a fair description of it as the basis for forming an opinion. One might say that this was one of the bases of good government for Mackenzie: that government action should be based on an understanding of public concerns through direct, first-person experience. Mackenzie never stated it as such, but his behaviour time and again showed that it is what he believed. The experiences he underwent frequently changed his political opinions. Such an approach is not always valued, since it can lead to different policies being voiced at different times, as though consistency were the least of concerns. One historian became so discouraged at plotting Mackenzie's policy changes in comparison with other Reformers as to conclude that "unlike Gourlay and land policy, Bidwell and the alien question, [Egerton] Ryerson and the Clergy Reserves, Baldwin and responsible government, Mackenzie never succeeded in taking the leadership on any prominent issue nor had he throughout his life a 'decided' policy." Mackenzie thought that responding to experience rather than reiterating predetermined solutions was the key policy worth pursuing.

In response to the new Tory majority, Mackenzie made a new alliance with the people of Upper Canada. In the summer of 1831 he travelled throughout the province to talk with people and listen to their concerns. In July he held many public meetings where the discussion focused on putting more power and control in the hands of the representatives of the colony, the secularization of the Clergy Reserves, achieving better control over the sale of public land, establishing powerful municipal councils (as was then being done in Britain), and ending the privileges of the Church of England. These issues were set down in a petition and signatures gathered, with the intention of making a direct appeal to the British government, as had been done successfully to pass the Naturalization Act a few years earlier. Mackenzie wrote of the empowering aspect of this process, which engaged the population directly in nineteen public meetings attended by several thousand residents. "The petitions to the King and Parliament will be signed by all classes," he claimed, "and simple means will be put into the hands of the General Committee in this town to enable them to fulfill the important duties which devolve on them.... THE FEW may continue to cry out, that wisdom remains with them, but THE MANY will cease to regard the voice of the charmer."

The petition began earnestly. Its first item of business was "That the qualified electors of the colony may be fairly and equally represented in the House of Assembly." Then followed the usual list of grievances.

On November 17, 1831, the assembly reconvened. Mackenzie went on the attack. In mid-December, the Tories decided they had had enough of his complaints and criticisms, and a new attempt was made to eject him from the Assembly. This time the complaint was that he had made a statement in the assembly that was "unfavourable to members of the House." The words Mackenzie had used ring out even these many years later: "sycophants," "mercenary," "subservience," "arbitrary," "despotic," and a derogatory comparison to the rulers of Russia:

> Our representative body has degenerated into a syco-
> phantic office for registering the decrees of as mean
> and mercenary an executive as ever was given as a
> punishment for the sins of any part of North America in
> the nineteenth century. We boast of our superior intelli-

gence, of our love of liberty; but where are the fruits? Has not the subservience of our legislation to a worthless executive become a by-word and a reproach throughout the colonies? Are we not now, even during the present week, about to give to the municipal officers of the government, as a banking monopoly, a power over the people, which, added to their already overgrown influence, must render their sway nearly as arbitrary and despotic as the iron rule of the Czar of Muscovy?

Last winter, the majority of our assembly, with our Speaker at their head, felt inclined to make contemptuous comparisons between the French inhabitants of a sister colony and the enlightened constituents who had returned them, the said majority. In our estimation, and judging of the tree by its fruits, the Lower Canadians are by far the most deserving population of the constitution they enjoy; for they show themselves aware of its value. While judging the people here by the representatives they return, it might be reasonably inferred that the constituents of the McLeans, Vankougnets, Jarvises, Robinsons, Burwells, Willsons, Boultons, MacNabs, McMartins, Frasers, Chisholms, Elliotts, Browns, Joneses, Masons, Samsons, and Hagermans had immigrated from Grand Tartary, Russia, or Algiers, the week proceeding the last general election; for, although in the turgid veins of their numbers, there be British blood, there certainly is not the appearance of much British feeling.

The Tories felt he had gone too far and should lose his place in the Assembly. Mackenzie had much to say in his own defence to the charge that these words should result in his expulsion — perhaps too much to say. His response in the assembly seems to have occupied several hours and fills the best part of thirty pages in one of his biographies. He used two main arguments. First, he noted that no law prevented him from voicing his own opinion even if his opinion is false, and that if such a law did exist, then discussion would be impossible: "If all false quotations and false opinions are improper, then all discussion, either in this House or through the press, must also be improper, for one set of opinions must be wrong. And if none but true opinions can be given or quoted by either party, then there can be no argument."

Second, he reiterated the position which led him to publish the *Advocate* in the first place: the need to inform people so they could reach their own conclusions. He asked, "How are the people to know when to approve or to disapprove of the conduct of their rulers, if the freedom of expressing all opinions concerning public men be checked?"

He then argued that if his opinions were improper, so were the opinions of those who recently criticized his actions and pinned various epithets on him, epithets which he repeated: "politico-religious juggler," "mock patriot," "contemptible being," "grovelling slanderer," "wandering impostor," one whose "censure is praise." He being blamed for "shameless falsehoods," "foul deeds,"

"envious malignity," and "impotent slanders." But he concluded, "All this it is expected I should quietly submit to,
and so I do."

He ended his argument in bitterness and resolve:

I must not call things by their right names in the newspaper called the *Advocate*; but either praise the most
undeserving of public men, be silent as death, or go
back to the freeholders of the country with the brand of
a "false, atrocious, and malicious libeller" on my fore-
head. If such shall be your measure of justice, I will not
shrink from the appeal to the country. Not one word,
not one syllable do I retract; I offer no apology; for
what you call libel I believe to be solemn truth, fit to be
published from one end of the province to the other.
I certainly should not have availed myself of my privilege, or made use of the language complained of on
this floor; but since I am called to avow or disavow that
language, as an independent public journalist I declare
I think it mild and gentle; for, be it remembered, Mr.
Speaker, I see for myself how matters are carried on
here; your proceedings are not retailed out to me at
second hand.

Powerful, convincing, and reasonable words, but not to
those who disagreed with him. On December 12, 1831, by
a vote of 24 to 15, the assembly declared Mackenzie "was
guilty of a high breach of the privileges of this House." He
was ejected, his seat was declared vacant, and a new

election was called. To nicely cap this exercise of Family Compact muscle, Attorney General Henry Boulton prolonged the name-calling by describing Mackenzie as a "reptile," a phrase that was amended and softened in the assembly's transcript by Solicitor General Alexander Hagerman to read "a spaniel dog."

The new election was set for January 2, 1832. The practice was to call for nominations, and then those entitled to vote would do so by openly and publicly declaring their choice. Mackenzie's biographer Charles Lindsey described the scene on January 2:

> Over two thousand persons were present. [At this time the population of the Town of York was less than 5,000.] There was a show of opposition to the re-election of Mackenzie. Mr. Street was nominated. Forty sleighs had come into town in the morning to escort Mackenzie to the polling place. An hour and a half after the poll opened, Mr. Street, having received one vote, against one hundred and nineteen cast for Mackenzie, abandoned the hopeless contest.

Mackenzie was back in the Assembly. But the problem of open and responsive government had not yet been resolved. On January 7, he was again ejected, this time for the publication of alleged "gross, slanderous, and malicious libels" in the *Advocate*, and the Tory majority declared that Mackenzie was incapable of holding a seat in the assembly. The assembly adjourned on January 28, two days before the next by-election was held.

In spite of the Assembly's declaration, Mackenzie offered himself as a candidate against a Tory and a moderate Reformer who ran on the assumption that Mackenzie was ineligible. The Tory withdrew after receiving 23 votes. The moderate received 96 votes, Mackenzie 628.

Since the assembly was not in session, Mackenzie returned to his task of public organizing. But as often occurs when government leaders belittle their opponents, the habit of denigrating opponents rubs off on others in society who are only too happy to be aggressive and offensive to those disliked by the rulers. On March 19, while in Hamilton to attend yet another public meeting, Mackenzie was lured to the door of the house where he was staying and was badly beaten by thugs, until rescued by neighbours. It is safe to assume the attackers were politically motivated. A few days later the windows of the *Advocate*'s office in Toronto were smashed during a street riot caused by Tory actions outside a meeting called by the Reformers. Mackenzie feared for his life and generally remained in hiding until he left for England in April, where he would present to the government the petition of grievances collected during the previous months. Isabel accompanied him on the journey, their three children being left in the care of his aging mother. Funding for the trip came from public subscription.

When he arrived in London in early June 1832, his interest in political intelligence was diverted by his experiences on the streets of the city:

The cries of London are among its greatest curiosities, and are greatly increased in number since I was last here. Sometimes half a dozen of persons are found within a stone's throw of each other, males and females, tenor and treble and bass voices, each bawling at the top of his or her voice something to be sold. I would consider such proceedings a perfect nuisance, did I not remember that in this day of misery and poverty, and hunger and disease and crime, many are driven to this means of earning an honest livelihood, for their aged parents, for their fatherless or motherless babes, for a sick wife, or a husband in prison or in difficulty. One of the cries is by a boy who comes along the street every day, once or twice, with a fine large milch cow, and milking pail and measure, bawling in a peculiar dialect "Milk! Milk from the Ka-u." To prevent suspicion of adulteration the process of milking is [per]formed in the middle of the street, in view of the customer. An Irishwoman, neatly dressed, passes daily, calling out in a musical strain, "Buy my water cresses;" and an active little dame often crosses her path, crying "any brooms wanted today, ma'am," in a tone between laughing and weeping. She addresses no one in particular; knocks at no door, but passes quickly along under her burthen.

With the intercession of the Scottish Radical member of Parliament Joseph Hume in London, Mackenzie had several meetings with Lord Goderich, who was responsible for colonial affairs. Mackenzie made a strong argument for more self-rule and provided a long written report which was the basis of an influential letter Goderich later sent to the government in Upper Canada. Meeting through Hume was a mixed blessing. It helped convince Lord Goderich of the justice of Mackenzie's cause, and in gratitude Mackenzie gave his son, born during the trip, the name Joseph Hume Mackenzie. Sadly, the child died in the fall of 1833, shortly after the family returned to Upper Canada.

But Hume's involvement alienated Egerton Ryerson, a fellow Reformer from Upper Canada. Ryerson, a strong Methodist, was visiting London at the same time to discuss a union of the Methodists with the British Wesleyans. The Wesleyans in Britain distrusted Hume, and Ryerson accepted the views of his English colleagues. He and other Methodists thought it better to declare for the liberals, then holding power, than for a Radical like Hume. That Mackenzie and Hume were working closely together meant that Ryerson had to break with Mackenzie.

There was one further issue which drove the men apart. The Methodists argued strongly for the separation of church and state — Mackenzie heartily agreed — but the British Wesleyans took a grant from the British government (for proselytizing to American Indians) and passed it on to the Upper Canadian Methodists, whose leader was Ryerson. Mackenzie scoffed loudly and publicly about the hypocrisy of the church taking this money from the state. Ryerson felt he had to protect his position, which he did in a letter published in October 1833, to the surprise and shock of Reformers in Upper Canada. It was

an enormously costly break although it could hardly have
been foreseen, since Ryerson had not made his position
clear to Mackenzie or any other Reformers in advance of
his public statement. When the rebellion occurred in
1837, the Methodists remained noncommittal or took the
lieutenant-governor's side against the rebels.

Mackenzie made special visits, as already noted, to
William Cobbett and to his publishing mentor, Robert
Rintoul, now editing the *Spectator*. He returned briefly to
Dundee to visit friends and settle an old debt from the
bankruptcy of his shop there. He was present in the House
of Lords for the third reading of the Reform Bill, which
promised real representation for the kinds of people
Mackenzie cared about. He convinced the government to
withhold approval of a bill from Upper Canada which
would have increased the capital stock of the Bank of
Upper Canada.

Back in Upper Canada, the Assembly reconvened on
October 31. One of the first orders of business was
Mackenzie's status. Attorney General Boulton and Solicitor General Hagerman both advised that the Assembly
had the power to decide who was eligible to be a member
— an "outrageous doctrine," averred one biographer —
and a majority of the assembly agreed. The results of the
January 30, 1832, election which had returned Mackenzie
were overturned, and a new by-election was set for
November 26. The indignation at the Tory decision was
such that no Tory candidate presented himself. Mackenzie,
still in Britain, was elected by acclamation.

It was at this point that Mackenzie's success in England with the colonial minister became clear. Lord Goderich instructed Lieutenant-Governor Colborne to publish his letter on proposed reforms in Upper Canada, and Colborne complied even though the tenor of Goderich's letter favoured the Reformers. Goderich agreed that town representatives in the Assembly would be paid an indemnity; that the requirement to swear oaths would be on the same footing as that used for Quakers, namely by affirmation; that public lands should be disposed of only by open competition; and that bishops and archdeacons should not hold political positions, such as on the Legislative and Executive Councils. He also favoured an independent judiciary. Tories were furious both that Goderich had met with Mackenzie, and that Mackenzie had been so successful in his arguments. The Assembly responded as though by rote: it once again expelled the absent Mackenzie.

In England, Mackenzie heard of the assembly's decision of early November to declare him ineligible to sit, and he pressed Goderich to take punitive action. Goderich immediately removed both Boulton and Hagerman from their posts. Hagerman was on his way to England when this decision was made and only learned of it when he arrived in London. He appealed to be reinstated and a newly appointed colonial minister, Lord Stanley, gave him his wish. Boulton came to England somewhat later and learned that the position of attorney general had been offered to someone else; and had to be satisfied with a posting to Newfoundland.

One can imagine Mackenzie's glee, not only that some of his arguments for reform had been successful but that the Tories had made such a mess of their position of strength. But the progress made was dampened by the appointment of the less supportive Lord Stanley. In response Mackenzie dropped "Colonial" from his paper's name in December. He returned to Upper Canada in the late summer of 1833, after fifteen months in Britain. Virtually his first action on return was to publish in the September 26, 1833, edition of the *Advocate*, his register of the colony's ruling faction, the Family Compact.

The Assembly reconvened on November 19. The majority refused Mackenzie his seat. Yet another election was called — Mackenzie's fifth in this one term of the Assembly — for December 17. He was again acclaimed. He came to the Assembly with a crowd of supporters who filled the gallery. They were rambunctious enough that the Speaker asked for the galleries to be cleared. Mackenzie refused to leave, saying that he was waiting to be sworn in. The sergeant-at-arms began to drag him out but was confronted by a burly supporter of Mackenzie. A more general melee ensued, the Speaker refused to permit Mackenzie to take the oath of office, and Mackenzie finally withdrew.

But the nonsense was not over. The next day the Assembly again accused Mackenzie of a libel, committed two years previous, and again ejected him. Mackenzie appealed to Lieutenant-Governor Colborne, who instructed the clerk of the Executive Council to administer the oath.

Mackenzie assumed his latest expulsion meant that taking the oath would have no effect, and he did nothing until friends convinced him to be sworn several months later. With the copy of the completed oath in his pocket, Mackenzie took his seat in the assembly on February 19, 1834. He was arrested by the sergeant-at-arms and the assembly fell into a tumultuous six-hour debate in which even Colborne was attacked by some Tories for supporting Mackenzie's rights. The arrest was rescinded, but once again Mackenzie was not permitted to sit in the Assembly.

The Assembly continued to sit, without Mackenzie, until it adjourned on March 6. The Tories had made such a symbol and popular hero of Mackenzie that they helped elevate him to the position he next held, the first mayor of the new city of Toronto.

6 · Mackenzie, First Mayor of Toronto

WHILE STILL IN England and away from the political fray, Mackenzie again addressed questions about the nature of politics and the role of the representative in a letter to a friend.

I have probably talked too much politics in my letters, but it should be remembered by the reader that politics is the science which teaches the people of a country to care for each other. If a mischievous individual were to attempt to cut off his neighbour's hand, would that neighbour's other hand and feet do well quietly to permit the amputation of the limb if they could hinder it?

All will say, No. This then is politics. That part of our
duty which teaches us to study the welfare of our whole
country, and not to rest satisfied altho' our own household is well off when our neighbours are in difficulty
and danger. The honest politician is he who gives all he
can of his time and means to promote the public good,
whose charity begins at home but does not end there.
The man who says he is no politician, is either ignorant
of what he is saying, or a contemptible selfish creature,
unworthy of the country or community of which he is
a part.

Back in Upper Canada he was buffetted by Tory winds
and kept from his elected post by decisions of a hostile
assembly, but he remained true to these values. When he
had the chance to serve the community, as mayor of the
new city of Toronto, he served well and promoted the
public good.

By 1834, York had grown to a population of more than
nine thousand, more than three times the population of
1831. The economy of Upper Canada had been booming
for more than a decade, and York saw the benefits. A new
brick market building had been constructed at King and
New (now Jarvis) Streets, and it included an auditorium
and a city hall. King Street was built up from Sherbourne
Street west to York Street, and beyond York Street were
impressive structures: the new Parliament Buildings at
Simcoe Street (replacing those near Berkeley Street
which had burned down) and Upper Canada College

across the street. A new courthouse and jail had been built near Church Street, and several new banks had opened offices. The town was awash in newspapers — seven in all, four of which were on the Reform side — and there was now a hospital, although it proved unable to cope with a deadly cholera epidemic in 1834.

The town was growing so quickly that the magistrates and constables appointed by the government were no longer able to provide effective decision-making or services to the citizens. Revenues were inadequate to meet needs. In Britain, the idea of municipal government had come into vogue, and legislators there were busy creating municipalities with their own powers and structures, independent of Parliament. It was thought that a municipal structure of some substance, established by but independent of the Assembly, was required for York. The problem — and it rears its head with every governmental reorganization — had to do with who would win power and who would lose control as a result of the changes. The Family Compact didn't want to effect a reorganization which would play into the hands of Mackenzie and his fellow Reformers.

The Reformers proposed a model for governing the town that they hoped would favour their supporters. They suggested that there be two kinds of council members: aldermen and councillors. Those with a relatively small property qualification could vote just for councillor; those with a more sizable property qualification could vote for alderman, councillor, and mayor. The Reformers also proposed a secret ballot rather than voting in public, with all of the pressure and intimidation that the latter involved.

For their part, the Tories thought the best way to frustrate the Reformers was by extending the vote to virtually all male residents, since Reform support was thought to be largely limited to middle-class property owners and not found among the newer and poorer Irish and Scottish immigrants, who were more amenable to a glass of whiskey or a small financial reward in return for their vote. This widening of the franchise — hardly a policy characteristic of Tories — was tempered and limited by the requirement of increased property qualifications for candidates. While more might be able to cast ballots, the persons they could vote for were substantial men of property who could be expected to do the right (Tory) thing. The Tories rejected the idea of a secret ballot and proposed that the mayor be elected by the council, not by voters. The Tories held a majority in the Assembly, and could not be stopped from putting this structure into legislation on March 6, 1833. It governed the first election for the new municipality, renamed Toronto.

The legislation expanded the municipal boundaries west to Dufferin Street, north to what came to be called Bloor Street, and east to the Don River. The city centre (generally the area defined by the current Bathurst, Dundas, and Parliament Streets, and the lake) was divided into five wards named after saints from the British Isles — Andrew, David, Patrick, and George — and Canada's patron saint, Lawrence. Each ward would elect

two aldermen and two councillors, making a council of
twenty members. Beyond these areas were the "liberties,"
the as yet unsettled areas.

The bill was contentious and brought objections from
both Reformers and some Tories. Mackenzie responded
to the Tory proposal in his usual fashion. He told his readers that the Tories were trying to keep information from
the public so that the populace would remain in the dark:

> In you is the power over the fortunes of the city
> vested, and according as the majority of you shall now
> decide will be the character and bearing of our future
> rulers. The Tories tell continually of your "ignorance,
> selfishness, habits of subjection and want of union";
> they call you "rabble" and trust that you will act as if
> you were such. They may find out their mistake! The
> reformers of Upper Canada expect you to come for-
> ward like men and like freemen — they confide fully in
> your intelligence, judgement and integrity."

Mackenzie, trusting the common people, said he would
give a plain account of the legislation reorganizing York in
the next issue of the *Advocate*, "and [as] it is the duty of
every good citizen to contribute his share to the common
fund of information I will afterwards print and distribute a
thousand extras, through the five wards." He concluded:

> Meantime I consider it of very great importance that
> the mechanics and labourers of the city and liberties

should hold a general preliminary meeting to give the act a careful consideration, so that it may be made to work the best for the general advantage; and for this purpose I invite you to assemble, in as great numbers as possible, at the Old King's Bench Court House in St. David's Ward, on Wednesday evening the 19th inst., at half past six o'clock, when ward committees of vigilance can be formed, and ward meetings arranged and provided for.

The election at the end of March didn't turn out the way the Compact hoped. Tory high-handedness in repeatedly ejecting Mackenzie from the assembly turned out to be the key issue of the city's election.

Mackenzie ran in St. David's Ward and secured an astounding 148 votes, by far the highest number of any candidate for alderman. Only Franklin Jackes, at 150 votes, and William Arthurs, at 161 votes, received higher totals, but they were both candidates for common councilman. Reformers generally did well and achieved a majority of seats on the first council of the new city. This was not the last time that those in power have tinkered with the voting system in the hope that it will produce results favourable to them. Instead, one might say it was the commencement of a long tradition which has continued unabated, with very mixed results. According to the Tory restructuring of the new city, it was the council majority's prerogative to select the mayor from among the aldermen elected. They selected Mackenzie as mayor by a vote of 10 to 8.

One historian writing at the city's sesquicentennial in 1984 noted, "It is hard for us to conceive how sorely it grated on the provincial establishment and its minions to see Mackenzie elected to the mayoralty, the first popular tribune in recent memory to occupy a prominent post of executive authority in the province." The establishment did not give Mackenzie or the Reform council an easy time. They criticized, attacked, and disrupted on every occasion they could.

The council and the mayor were both faced with challenges which would have been difficult to resolve easily in the best of times. For one thing, the municipality's financial position was weak. Before the city was restructured, the magistrates who had responsibility for providing services had at their disposal only the inadequate revenue from a property tax levied at the rate of one penny per pound of assessed value. When the magistrates had to build a new jail and courthouse in the 1820s, that project put them in debt. The construction of a new market only intensified the financial strain. The provincial restructuring legislation required the new city to assume these financial burdens from the former town. At the same time some provincial financial responsibilities were transferred to the new council. As in the amalgamation of Toronto in 1998, the ability of the municipality to address its financial problems was constrained by provincial rules and regulations, particularly unfair property assessment and property tax provisions.

Aggravating these difficulties was the need to make costly improvements to the city. New sewers were badly needed, as were wooden sidewalks, and both came at a price. Legislation permitted the new council to levy taxes as high as four pence per pound of assessed value, but the Reform council shied away from such a heavy tax. The assessment system was unfair, grossly undervaluing substantial properties and structures owned by the Family Compact, so that the taxes paid by those well-to-do owners were little higher than those paid by owners of very modest means. Yet the revenue was required. In view of the assessment problem, a rate of two pence was settled on, although even that rate was met by cynical opposition from the Tory councillors.

Although there was considerable concern about borrowing to meet the cost as to way to find money, council authorized borrowing one thousand pounds for road repairs. The loan request was turned down by the Bank of Upper Canada and other established financial institutions controlled by friends of the Family Compact — they had no wish to help the Reform majority make a success of its role. Finally a newly formed Toronto partnership agreed to take the loan.

Another source of contention was that many of the elections to council were contested, and it was council's job to sort out who would be declared elected and who would not. Despite spirited criticism from the Tory press, Mackenzie — who as mayor chaired the process — made the sensible decision that those whose elections were contested would not be permitted to vote in their own interest. These matters were eventually resolved in a satisfactory manner.

In spite of these challenges, council overcame the problems of creating a new municipal structure *ex nihilo*. It established standing committees which functioned well. It passed bylaws in its first few months of operation to deal with critical issues such as establishing a board of health, legislating standards of fire prevention, controlling of nuisances, regulating markets, and establishing the position of treasurer.

As mayor, Mackenzie also served in two positions as a judge. One role was as chief magistrate of the mayor's court, which met every few months to handle significant criminal matters. Another was as a member of the police court, which met almost daily, making decisions about offences considered more minor, such as drunkenness, disorderly conduct, wife beating, and liquor offences. Mackenzie was not a lawyer; he was a journalist and politician used to having opinions and taking sides. Impartial mediation was hardly his strength. Yet while he performed this judging role reasonably well, the public naturally treated him like a politician and came to political conclusions about his decisions. The Tory press complained that his sentences were either too lenient or too strict. One decision that created considerable Tory outrage was his consignment of a woman, reported to be habitually intoxicated, to the stocks for insulting him in the courtroom.

Mackenzie continued to publish his newspaper while
mayor, and that led to another crisis. Joseph Hume sent
the *Advocate* a letter commenting on Mackenzie's expulsion from the Assembly the previous December. Hume
said that the event would "hasten that crisis which will
terminate in independence and freedom from baneful
domination of the Mother Country and the tyrannical conduct of a small and despicable fraction of the colony."
When the letter was published in the *Advocate* on May 22,
it caused an uproar. The Tories interpreted "baneful domination" as an attack on all that they held dear and attrib-
uted the demeaning sentiment to Mackenzie as the publisher of the paper. They mounted considerable political
pressure (a provincial election was expected momentarily),
and Mackenzie responded in July with public meetings to
voice complaints about the limited powers under which
the new city had to function. Mackenzie's speech on one
occasion went on for so long that the meeting, held in the
market, was adjourned until the next day, when Sheriff
Samuel Jarvis spoke in reply. During Jarvis's speech the
gallery collapsed and four people were killed. The Tory
press blamed Mackenzie for the tragedy.

At the end of July an outbreak of cholera occurred,
more powerful than the 1832 epidemic, and five hundred
residents of Toronto died. City council ceased meeting
during the summer. Mackenzie, like his arch-enemy Dr.
John Strachan, spent time taking the sick to the hospital.
Mackenzie himself became ill. The city's population was
less than ten thousand at this point, so the death toll was

significant, in the order of 5 per cent of all residents.

The provincial election was held in October. The County of York was now divided into four ridings. Mackenzie was a candidate in one of them and was re-elected with 334 votes, overwhelming Edward Thomson with 178 votes. Since the Assembly did not start meeting until early in 1835, he continued serving as mayor. The city council meetings became somewhat chaotic once it appeared the Assembly would once more have a Reform majority. It would be unfair to blame this chaos entirely on Mackenzie and the Reformers: the Tories, now seeing themselves in the minority in both governments, did much to make the situation unmanageable, including denying the council a quorum on several occasions.

Mackenzie was unwillingly nominated for alderman for St. David's Ward, and when the city election occurred early in 1835, he did nothing in his own cause and was not elected. He did not see this as a setback, since in fact his wish was to return to the provincial scene.

There is considerable contention among historians about the success or otherwise of Mackenzie's term as mayor. Some argue that it shows he was more suited to opposing than to administering, although he appears to have done reasonably well at the latter tasks. It was the one time when Mackenzie was in a position of considerable power *inside* government, but it was a restructured government not of the Reformers' making, hedged round by many Tory constraints. The very worst one could say is that Mackenzie was seen to be better at being a catalyst for change than an administrator. He was certainly not a failure. One historian noted "Mackenzie proves to have been a hard-working mayor who conducted an honest administration and got Toronto's municipal existence off to a reasonably good start."

Certainly the mayoralty did not reveal any hitherto hidden flaws in his character. He continued to exhibit the same interest he always had in using first-hand experience to shape his opinions. One of his first acts as mayor was to tour the city's slums with city officials, seeing for himself, gambling, selling of unlicensed alcohol, and "vice in its blackest shapes."

No one has accused Mackenzie of misusing his position as mayor or of besmirching his strong values while in a position of power. In fact he refused to wear the fancy regalia of the office and insisted that his salary be kept at the minimum allowed by provincial legislation, 100 pounds, even though 250 pounds had been recommended by one city committee. He said the salary should remain low until the unfair assessment law was changed. His social modesty was entirely in character.

In late 1834 there was an attempt to establish a unified Reform organization. A meeting was held in Toronto on December 9, where the Canadian Alliance Society was created under the slogan "When bad men conspire, good men must unite." Those present at the meeting agreed to form a society with branches throughout Canada and appointed Mackenzie as the corresponding secretary. The objectives of the society stretched for twenty-three points:

responsible, representative government and the abolition of the Legislative Council; the prevention of a legislative union of Upper and Lower Canada; vote by secret ballot; separation of church and state; the sale of the Clergy Reserves; a less complicated and expensive system of legal procedures; a free press and better libel laws; and more control over local matters.

But the Canadian Alliance didn't go very far, meeting on only a few more occasions before disappearing altogether. (The irony of the party names "Reform" and "Alliance" at the end of the millennium is remarkable.) The meetings may have clarified issues once again, but they were not able to create a cohesive team of Reformers. Even if the Reformers agreed on the nature of an issue, they often differed about the strategy to be used, which meant that each issue was resolved on its own merits. The Family Compact acted as a cohesive entity and was effective. The Tories were relatively united, although their interests did not always coincide with those of the elite or the Family Compact. In contrast, the Reformers constituted a loose coalition of individuals sharing many political beliefs about the meaning of good government, and for that and other reasons were less effective. Mackenzie's newspapers provided a focus for those who believed there should be change in Upper Canada, and did much to popularize a Reform position. But Mackenzie asked for debate and discussion to arrive at strong positions, not party adherence. Returning to the assembly, Mackenzie prepared himself for pushing the Reform agenda ahead.

7 · Grievances Unresolved

THE PROVINCIAL ELECTION in late 1834 had given another majority to the Reformers. When the new assembly convened early in 1835, Marshall Bidwell was again elected Speaker — as he had been in 1828 — and Mackenzie was appointed chair of the Committee on Grievances. He immediately set the committee to work, calling the first witnesses before the committee in early February.

Mackenzie used the Grievances Committee as a forum to address many concerns, giving members of the public the chance to talk openly about the problems they faced. There were three kinds of witnesses, as the preface to the committee's *Seventh Report* noted. The first, "of whom the Venerable Dr. Strachan is one," was "of the opinion that the Government is well enough as it is, and that as to responsibility it is as responsible as other Governments." In short, this was the Family Compact position. The second kind of witnesses were those who believed in responsible government: that is, government business directed by the will of the majority of elected members. The report noted that "this system was never attempted in any of the old colonies," but "with some modifications it might be productive of a greater share of good government and public prosperity than is at present enjoyed by the people." The third kind of witnesses favoured the American example of using elections to fill important position such as judgeships. The second group described the position favoured by many Reformers; but as to the American approach, even Mackenzie appeared ambivalent.

The committee gave Mackenzie a forum for raising embarrassing questions and forcing members of the Family Compact to answer under-oath questions about their relationships to the government. He interrogated an official of the Canada Company, the private corporation which purchased land from the Crown at very low prices and sold it for substantially higher ones to new immigrants. Testimony began several days a week, continuing from early February until early April 1835, and then the committee issued its report.

Two thousand copies of the *Seventh Report of the Grievance Committee* were printed in late spring 1835 and widely circulated. The fifty-page forward or preface

appears to have been written by Mackenzie, and it was
followed by verbatim transcripts of testimony from several dozen witnesses before the committee, followed in
turn by a multitude of letters to and from Mackenzie as
committee chair, concerning the business of the committee, and Lord Goderich's letter to Colborne of 1831. The
report made no recommendations, although the preface
sums up the main argument, which was for independent
self-government to ensure that Upper Canada was governed well. The preface noted that a similar government
committee had reported in 1828, and that it had expected
no improvement "unless an impartial, conciliatory and
constitutional system of government be observed in these
loyal and important colonies."

The report made the argument for self-government by
exposing extravagant patronage and the inability of current decision-makers to understand the critical changes
required for reasonable efficiency in governing Upper
Canada. "The almost unlimited extent of the patronage of
the Crown, or rather of the Colonial Minister for the time
being and his advisers here, together with the abuse of
that patronage, are the chief sources of colonial discontent." It documented the patronage, including long lists of
the amounts of money received by various individuals as
gifts, salaries, and pensions, and specifically argued that
patronage coloured the operation of the judicial system. It
noted that the Crown's representatives were responsible
for important appointments in virtually all sectors of the
province's economic and social life, including fifteen

hundred commissioned militia officers. Further, "The Crown also controls the expenditure of a large annual amount of local taxation by its power of appointing the District Magistracy during its pleasure — the justices thus appointed select the District Treasurers and a large number of subordinate officers, and exercise varied and extensive civil and criminal jurisdiction." Some of these appointees refused to account for their expenses. The report was specific about the amounts of money consumed by this patronage, complaining that it was raised in Canada (not paid from Britain) and was a considerable drain on the finances of the colony. At a time when the total population of Upper Canada did not exceed two hundred thousand, patronage amounted "at least to £50,000 a year (exclusive of the Clergy Grants), the whole being raised from the people themselves and not one farthing derived from England." Some of that public money went to clergymen from the Church of England.

A list of who received what was included. About 125 individuals received more than 100 pounds a year — enough to make a family quite well off — and almost an equal number under 100 pounds. "Upwards of £38,000 have been paid from the Colonial Revenues within the last eight years to the Lieutenant Governors, the greater part of which it is probable they save and carry to Europe." In comparison, "the incomes of Governors in the northern parts of the [United] States vary from £100 to £1500 a year, and the incumbents are taken from among the resident inhabitants." The lieutenant-governor at the time, Sir

John Colborne, received 5,631 pounds a year, and his private secretary 808 pounds. The report noted, regarding the secretary: "It appears to us that this office ought to be done away with, and the duties performed by the existing public departments which are abundantly sufficient for their discharge."

The Grievances Committee documented the patronage that was sullying institutions that should be free of it, such as the Canada Company and companies established for banking and building canals, docks, and wharves. The report noted that the post office generated a surplus which was sent to England and that postage rates were "extravagant" compared with those in the United States; it urged change that would "give the Colonists the entire control of this Department in Upper Canada."

The report was very disparaging about the Legislative Council, appointed by the lieutenant-governor with power to block decisions of the popularly elected body, the Legislative Assembly. It concluded that the relationship between the Legislative Council and the justice system, through the person of the chief justice, was entirely wrong: "We have already adverted to the circumstance of the Chief Justice being introduced into the Legislative Council, of which he is Speaker (and paid a salary of £200 per year for this position); and although the House of Assembly has repeatedly pointed out to His Majesty's Government, the inexpediency, in a limited community like this, of blending the judicial and political duties together, yet the same injurious system is continued. Its impropriety has been lately manifested by the result of a pecuniary negotiation likely to seriously impair the independence of the judiciary and increase the distrust of the people."

One British statesman, the committee maintained, described the Legislative Council as being "at the root of all the evils complained of in both Provinces" and concluded with a call for its replacement by an elected body, perhaps (although not specified) like the American senate: "It appears therefore that the Legislative Council, as at present constituted, has utterly failed, and never can be made to answer the ends for which it was created; and the restoration of legislative harmony and good government requires its reconstruction on the elective principle."

Similar criticisms were made of the Executive Council, the body appointed by the lieutenant-governor as his personal cabinet, and of the inappropriateness of putting so many decisions in the hands of the lieutenant-governor. These arguments went to the heart of the need for independent self-government for Upper Canada.

> The affairs of this country have been ... subjected in the most injurious manner to the interferences and interdictions of a succession of Colonial ministers in England who have never visited the country, and can never possibly become acquainted with the state of parties, or the conduct of public functionaries, except through official channels in the province which are illy calculated to convey the information necessary to dis-

close official delinquencies and correct public abuses. A painful experience has proved how impracticable it is for such a succession of strangers beneficially to direct and control the affairs of the people 4000 miles off; and being an impracticable system, felt to be intolerable by those for whose good it was professedly intended, it ought to be abolished, and the domestic institutions of the province so improved and administered by the local authorities as to render the people happy and contented.

Such a system of government, securing to the people inestimable blessings, would rather durably enlarge than impair the commercial relations with the parent state, in exchange for which we receive protection; and could in no wise prejudicially affect any benefits now yielded to her, except the loss, if loss it can be called, of that patronage the partial and impolitic distribution of which has ever proved unsatisfactory and injurious to the colony.

The report then took direct aim at the position of lieutenant-governor, stating, "Men, from the too long possession of lucrative power, whatever at first might be their relative stations soon acquire a community of interests, and thus identified in the purpose of sustaining each other in office, they have in this province made common cause against that redress of our grievances, and that conciliation of the public mind, and that economy of the public wealth, which are equally dictated by justice and wisdom."

The conclusion laid out the committee's key proposal, for powers to be vested in the elected representatives of the people as embodied in the House of Assembly, stated with a rather touching humility.

The House of Assembly has, at all times, made satisfactory provision for the civil government, out of the revenues raised from the people by taxation, and while there is cherished an unimpaired and continued disposition to do so, it is a reasonable request that His Majesty's adviser in the province and those about him should possess and be entitled to the confidence of the people and their representatives, and that all their reasonable wishes respecting their domestic institutions and affairs should be attended to and complied with.

It was a powerful report, but no one expected immediate redress. Mackenzie turned his energies to the next matter at hand, an examination of the precarious and somewhat scandalous accounts of the Welland Canal, a private project in which the government of Upper Canada had invested public funds.

Mackenzie had some small experience with canals, and the assembly appointed him in 1835 as a director of the Welland Canal Company. He supported the building of the Welland Canal to provide passage around Niagara Falls, but he had little good to say about the way the undertaking was proceeding or about the patronage that was involved.

Before the end of the year the *Seventh Report of the Grievances Committee* was laid before senior officials in Britain. That they were obviously impressed can be seen by their action: they summarily dismissed the lieutenant-governor. On the eve of his return to Britain in what he may have seen as his last hurrah, Colborne made a grant of seventy-seven thousand acres of land to the Church of England in Canada for the construction of forty-four new rectories. The giveaway inflamed public opinion.

In the midst of this contretemps, Colborne's replacement, Sir Francis Bond Head, arrived in Toronto in January 1836. Head had no political experience and had not been in Canada before, but he wanted to make a strong and positive impression. Head sought to show his independence in this new office by making careful appointments to his powerful Executive Council. He set out to conciliate local interests by reaching out to government critics as his advisers. Three moderates — Robert Baldwin, John Rolph (who in 1834 had not run for re-election to the Assembly), and John Henry Dunn — were appointed in mid-February to fill vacancies and join the three Tories.

Baldwin was a firm believer in the kind of responsible government expressed by the second class of people who gave testimony to the Grievances Committee. He was also respectable and persuasive. He convinced his five colleagues on the Executive Council that the council should tell Head that they expected to be consulted by him on all administrative and policy matters.

It was an audacious proposal which, if agreed to, would calmly take Upper Canada a considerable distance along the road to responsible government, requiring the lieutenant-governor to consult before taking action. The recommendation was made on March 4. Six days later, Head angrily rejected it. On March 12, all six resigned. On March 14, the assembly voted 53 to 2 for "a responsible Executive Council to advise the Lieutenant Governor on the Affairs of the province." Head immediately appointed four men to the Executive Council, but the Assembly was not assuaged. On March 24, a motion of want of confidence in the new council carried the Assembly by a vote of 32 to 19.

In April the Assembly members in their anger took a very sizable step: they refused to approve the supply bill which provided salaries and pensions for virtually all government employees. Head responded in turn by refusing to sign the bills passed by the Assembly, effectively halting its ambitious public works program for building schools and roads. The result was public inaction and further financial distress, which intensified an already worrisome economic crisis. Unemployment was rising and trade falling across the province.

The Assembly was prorogued by Head in April and dissolved in May, and an election was quickly called for June. Reformers gathered under the banner of a new group, the Constitutional Reform Society. The society adopted an agenda similar to that set out in the *Seventh Report of the Committee on Grievances*: an elected

Legislative Council; an Executive Council responsible to public opinion; revenue to be in the control of the Assembly; and no interference in local affairs by the colonial officials in Britain.

Although Head, as the Crown's representative, was expected to stay out of local politics, he played a forward role in this election, blaming the Reformers for all the problems. The election was marked by extremely combative language from Head and his supporters, and there were many allegations of vote rigging and threats of violence against Reform candidates and supporters. One Reformer cited Head's improper election activity as a cause for the rebellion a year later:

All along we expected to straighten things out at the polls until Sir Francis and his crowd swamped us out in the election in the summer of 1836. Why, his men distributed tickets giving titles to farms on the shore road and the bush that no one ever knew were farms. With these tickets in their hands the hired men would go to the polls and swear that they got four dollars a year out of farms they did not own nor no one else ever did own. But these ticket holders swore enough votes through to beat us Reformers who had property in the country, and after that we saw that there was nothing before us but a fight.

Reports of intimidation came from London, in the southwest:

If you had been in London at the last election, you would have seen a set of government tools called Orange men running up and down the streets crying five pounds for a liberal; and if a man said contrary to their opinion he was knocked down. Many were knocked down in this way and others were threatened; and all this in the presence of magistrates, Church of England ministers and judges, who made use of no means to prevent such outrages.

"Tory votes were manufactured wholesale, and Tory funds were squandered with reckless profusion," wrote one historian, "Gangs of ruffians were stationed at the polls to intimidate those who ventured near to record their votes in favour of anti-government candidates."

These strong-arm tactics proved largely successful. Head and his Tory forces carried the day. "Demagogy, threats, intimidation at the polls, gangsterism, all combined to give Sir Francis his desired majority," concluded one historian. The Reformers were roundly defeated. Other factors may have also been at play. Following the lead of Egerton Ryerson when he distanced himself from the Reform cause, many Methodists voted for Tory candidates. Some think that Mackenzie's publication of Hume's letter two years earlier, about "baneful domination" may have convinced some voters that Reformers secretly intended on separating from Britain. Rolph ran and was returned, but Mackenzie was not re-elected: it seems Head and the Tories had gone to special lengths to ensure his defeat.

Mackenzie was devastated. He had always shown moody spells, but this was a transforming event. Regaining his bearings, he responded by forming a new newspaper, the *Constitution*, with his son James as the printer. He again needed a device to speak out and encourage public debate. The *Constitution* was first published on July 4, 1836, the sixtieth anniversary of the American revolution, a date not chosen at random.

At the end of the year, Mackenzie lodged a petition of complaint against the man who had ousted him in the election, Edward Thomson, and produced evidence that would probably have overturned the results. But Mackenzie was given bad advice by the clerk and failed to file another document within the prescribed time period, and the petition failed on this technicality.

At this time, the American economy was in some difficulty, and economic gloom gathered in Upper Canada, compounding the effect of Head's decision to disallow the program of public works. Mackenzie relied again on the device he thought was the foundation of good, responsive government: public meetings. He helped organize them throughout the province to discuss what might be done. It was the medicine he needed to revive his spirits, as he noted in early February 1837: "I have constantly identified myself with the common people of the country, have earnestly and anxiously sought to raise them higher and higher in the scale of intelligence, and will yet venture to believe with the Ayrshire Ploughman, that instead of encouraging Orange Lodges, Established Priesthoods,

close Corporations, and delegated Tyrannies, mankind
will become brotherly-minded. What else but this hope
could have supported me through the struggles of the last
fifteen years?" He also turned to his business interests,
which had prospered in the past several years, travelling
to New York in March to make purchases for his publishing company.

Then came another political blow. In March 1837, Lord
Russell, the English prime minister and moving force of
reform in Britain, received the support of the House of
Commons for his "Ten Resolutions." This document opposed
the idea of responsible government in Upper Canada and
confirmed the central control of the lieutenant-governor
and his advisers, unfettered by elected representatives.
Mackenzie had held out hopes for the English reformers
since his visit to England a few years earlier, but now that
hope was crushed.

Mackenzie counselled more public meetings and public
discussion to seek a way forward. "The best course to
pursue at this crisis," he wrote in May 1837, "would be
to call a Convention of the people of Upper and Lower
Canada, to devise means to rescue the country from its
present distressed state. The mock parliaments of the
colonial office do not represent the intelligence, wealth
and population of Upper Canada.... But a convention of
the provinces, if properly attended, will be the salvation
of our common country. Head and his folks have had trial
enough now; their measures excite a mingled feeling of
indignation, derision and contempt. Farmers and mechan-

ics, you must look to yourselves — be honest and united
and the day is won."

His intention was to call together everyone who produced the wealth of the country, "the true source of a
country's wealth — labour usefully and prudently applied."
He produced an exhaustive list of who those wealth-
makers might be — excluding, of course, bankers, who he
felt did more harm than good. The list provides a fine
snapshot of the economic and social life of the society in
which he lived and fairly describes the broad constituency
Mackenzie and other Reformers relied on for support and
direction. Women were given a central role, although mostly as helpmates to the men. The document also outlines
Mackenzie's view that government was an institution
whose purpose was to help citizens generate wealth.

To produce this wealth, the Farmer, the Miller, the
Labourer, the Sailor, the Merchant, each contributes
his share, by useful industry in an honest calling. The
Weaver, too, and the Tailor, and the Shoemaker, and
the Hatter, and the Smith, and the Wagon Maker, the
Teamster, the Ship Carpenter, the Millwright, the
Sawyer, the Mason, the House Carpenter, the Cooper,
the Schoolmaster, and the Government lend their bene-
ficial aid. The Farmer is up late and early, ploughing
and sowing, and fulfilling the duties of a Husbandman
— the Miller carefully prepares the grain for food —
the Cooper curiously fashions and hoops the barrels
which are to convey this food to the consumer —

the labourer prepares the highway for man's use, and toils with the Mason, the Smith and other craftsmen, powerfully assisting them by the strength of his arm and with the sweat of his brow — the Tailor, Hatter and Shoemaker clothe the body to preserve it from the inclemency of the weather, and its great hat to keep the head from the cold of winter or the feverish excitement which might be produced by the heat of the summer's sun, and the feet comfortable under all the vicissitudes of the seasons — the steamer and schooner plough the sea or the lake to bear the food of man to the desired port — the merchant ships the produce, makes himself acquainted with the usages of other lands, their coins, their customs' duties, their most upright traders, ascertains who are the most trusty ship captains, what steamers or other vessels are the most sea-worthy, and the state of the markets — and the schoolmaster by his precept and example, and opening to the view of delighted and astonished youth the history of the past, endeavours to prepare them for enacting with honour, usefulness and integrity their respective parts in the work of this world, in which they are so soon to be called to take a share. Nor should I forget the Minister of Religion — he too is most useful, if he remind his fellow men at fit and convenient seasons, of the great and awful truth that they are but pilgrims and strangers here, seeking another and a better country, and looking forward to the enjoyment of happiness which this unstable world never can, never will afford.

In exhibiting the sources of wealth, I do not forget the important share of labour performed by woman. She is the nurse of infancy, a guardian in youth, a comforter in age and sickness. She prepares the food of man — she watches over his tender years — she preserves order and cleanliness through all her household — she smoothes down the asperities of life, and is the ornament alike of the palace and the cottage.

The multitude of people with different skills and concerns were the Canadians of "honest industry" who Mackenzie hoped would rise in "stern and awful majesty, and demand in strange tones their ever despised and hitherto denied rights. They rise and swear in a deep and startling oath that Justice Shall Reign."

The way ahead was not clear for Mackenzie or any other of the Reformers in Upper Canada. Something needed to be done, but what that was had not yet been determined.

8 · The Rebellion Fails

UNDER MACKENZIE'S PRODDING, large public meetings were held throughout Upper Canada in the summer and early fall of 1837, organizing opposition to the government. Three or four dozen meetings were held and Mackenzie was present at most of them. The meetings endorsed resolutions in support of self-government, and generally concluded with the formation of local Vigilance Committees.

The excitement created by these meetings must have been electric. Mackenzie had the good sense to write about them, setting them in a larger context about the nature of power and change. The result was a powerful

analysis not often seen in his writings, outlining general
social trends that were large enough to overcome individual idiosyncrasies.

Canadians! It has been said that we are on the verge
of a revolution. We are in the midst of one; a bloodless
one, I hope, but a revolution to which all those who
have been [part] will be counted mere child's play.
Calm as society may seem to a superficial spectator, I
know that it is moved to its very foundations, and is in
universal agitation.

The question which is now debated, and to which
entire humanity listens, is one which reaches infinitely
further than the most celebrated of the questions
heretofore debated. The question today is not between
one reigning family and another, between one people
and another, between one form of government and
another, but a question between privilege and equal
rights, between law sanctioned, law fenced in privilege,
age-consecrated privilege, and a hitherto unheard-of
power, a new power just started from the darkness in
which it has slumbered since creation day, the *Power of
Honest Industry*.

The strange name borne by this new-born power,
may deceive some as to its strength and merits, but
though they may deem it an infant, they may be assured
they will find it a Herculean one. The contest is now
between the privileged and the unprivileged, and a terrible one it is. The slave snaps his fetters, the peasant
feels an unwonted strength nerve in his arm, the people

rise in stern and awful majesty, and demand in strange tones their ever despised and hitherto denied rights. They rise and swear in a deep and startling oath that *Justice Shall Reign.* Not to this country and continent alone, nor chiefly, is this revolution confined. It reaches the old world. The millions down-trodden for ages by kings, hierarchies, and nobilities, awake. Kings put their hands to their heads if their crowns be there; hierarchies lash themselves and cry mightily into Baal; nobilities tremble for their privileges; time-cemented and moss-covered state fabrics reel and totter; all who live on abuses seem to themselves to see the hand-writing on the walls of their palaces, and to feel *Every Thing Giving Way Beneath Them.*

These were extraordinary images that Mackenzie painted, far beyond the normal scope of his comments. He linked the emerging order with justice of a biblical sort descending from high poetry, then ended with the compelling cartoon of the lieutenant-governor of the day, Sir Francis Bond Head, sitting on a throne in the wilderness of Upper Canada: "Aye, and the puffed up, angry little creature, who sits perched upon a mahogany throne in a chamber up here in Toronto, playing the petty tyrant of an hour, might as well borrow Dame Partington's mop wherewith she sought to stay the ocean's swelling tide, as attempt to uphold the odious system of swindling, plunder, speculation and official robbery, whether by law or without it of which the many so deeply and bitterly complain."

One document that fairly summed up the discontents fuelling the rebellious mood was the "Declaration of Reformers" adopted at a Toronto meeting in early August 1837. It started with a general statement of principles and soon slipped into a lengthy and somewhat tedious recitation of familiar grievances, ending with calls of solidarity with reformers in Lower Canada and a rather convoluted motion from Mackenzie about self-government. Those looking for revolutionary fervour will not find it here. The declaration bore many similarities to the language in the *Seventh Report of the Grievances Committee*, and in all likelihood it was also from Mackenzie's hand. It began with the now common argument that government is for the benefit of ordinary people, and therefore "people have a natural right given them by their Creator to seek after and establish such institutions as will yield the greatest quantity of happiness to the greatest number." It noted that grievances voiced had not been rectified and that those who made decisions were many miles removed from Upper Canada. It used the phrase from Joseph Hume that so infuriated the Family Compact: "This system of baneful domination has been uniformly furthered by a Lieutenant Governor sent amongst us as an uninformed, unsympathising stranger." The declaration complained, "we have been insulted, injured and reduced to the brink of ruin. The due influence and purity of all our institutions have been utterly destroyed."

The ending of the document was somewhat inconclusive, reflecting the fact that no one had a clear idea of what exactly should happen next. The first resolution was a statement of thanks and admiration to the patriots in Lower Canada, in particular Louis-Joseph Papineau, "for their present devoted, honorable and patriotic opposition to the attempt of the British government to violate their constitution without their consent."

The second resolution stated that Reformers in Upper Canada should "make common cause with their fellow citizens of Lower Canada" by calling public meetings throughout the province, and that a convention of delegates should be held in Toronto to appoint leaders to converse with their counterparts in Lower Canada. A third, rather muddled resolution implied that the basis for opposing the government was its unwillingness to endorse free trade.

There was no talk of organized violence at these meetings, nor of a general uprising. True, some of those attending brought pikes, muskets, pistols, and clubs, but that was for protection from Orangemen who, having been given a mandate at the last general election by Head to harass reform-minded citizens, offered real threats, including at least one threat on Mackenzie's life.

It is unclear exactly what Mackenzie or other leaders expected would occur next. Opinion is unanimous that he did not talk publicly at these meetings, nor privately among his supporters, of rebellion or armed uprising. He and others might have voiced general threats to the established order but there was no organizing activity making such threats a reality. As usual, he seemed to rely on the power of public discussion by the citizenry as the device which would find a way forward.

Mackenzie made several visits in the early fall to Lower Canada and Quebec, and working relations were forged between Upper Canada reformers and those in Lower Canada. The rebels in Lower Canada, the Upper Canadians learned, were much better organized and their participants clearer about their strategies, including open rebellion. These meetings may have been a significant influence on the course finally determined for Upper Canada.

October through November was a period of active organizing in Upper Canada. The first mention of rebellion was probably made in late October, and support was expressed by John Rolph, Dr. T.D. Morrison, and Silas Fletcher. Jesse Lloyd was sent to Lower Canada in the second week of November both to convey plans of the uprising to French-Canadian rebels and to learn of their plans. Mackenzie went to the smaller communities north of Toronto and on some occasions was perhaps too optimistic, according to his Toronto colleagues, about the ease with which the grand rebellious events would unfold. Mackenzie held a meeting in the third week of November in Toronto with the key rebels, including Samuel Lount, Jesse Lloyd, Silas Fletcher, James Bolton, Nelson Gorham, and Peter Matthews. Rolph and Morrison were concerned about the degree of support in the countryside, but Mackenzie assured them, certainly overconfidently, that it was significant. At this meeting, the date of December 7 was set for the uprising. Little else was settled, save that the rebels would gather north of Toronto and march on the city.

It seems no serious options were being discussed other than open rebellion, and given the need to move opinion forward, one wonders whether, when this kind of climax was presenting itself in Lower Canada, there was simply no turning back from a similar outcome in Upper Canada. Kilbourn suggests Mackenzie was following the lesson from Joseph Hume in Britain: "without a display of physical force there would have been no Reform Bill."

On November 23, the first violent engagement in Lower Canada occurred between British authorities and Quebec rebels, with victory going to the rebels. It is unlikely that Mackenzie would have learned of this for some days: after the date-setting meeting he had headed north once more. On November 27, Mackenzie published a broadsheet signalling a call to arms. It was not circulated in Toronto, only in communities around the city.

The broadsheet contained a list of common grievances (again) and a call to arms. It relied on some very tired tactics, such as promising financial reward if success is achieved. It demonized the enemy, recounting the Family Compact's evil qualities, and like many other revolutionary documents of the time it exhibited a pious reliance on the Almighty as the source of victory. Yet almost two centuries later it remains extraordinarily clear and accessible.

The details of the incident referred to in the last paragraph of the broadsheet are uncertain. George Gurnett was a stalwart Tory and during 1837 was Toronto's mayor. Mackenzie appeared to be alleging that Gurnett, as mayor and chief magistrate, arrested the sons of Mackenzie's colleague Joseph Sheppard on trumped-up charges at the instigation of Sir Francis Bond Head.

The rousing lines that have become closely associated with Mackenzie — "Canadians! Do you love freedom? I know you do! Do you hate oppression? Who dare deny it?" — began the second paragraph. The frequent biblical references are those that were well known to everyone in the 1830s and needed no explanation at the time. The tone of the document was bold, the purpose is obvious — yet there's some uncertainty as to exactly what people were expected to do next, as though it was a general call to arms subject to instructions which would come later. Mackenzie may have been trying to do two things at once: issue instructions about the uprising to supporters, yet hide critical details of the rebellion from Head's forces. Or he may have had continuing reluctance to committing himself to the next steps.

> BRAVE CANADIANS! God has put into the bold and honest hearts of our brethren in Lower Canada to revolt — not against "lawful" but against "unlawful" authority." The law says we shall not be taxed without our consent by the voices of the men of our choice, but a wicked and tyrannical government has trampled upon

that law — robbed the exchequer — divided the plunder — and declared that, regardless of justice they will continue to roll their splendid carriages, and riot in their palaces, at our expense — that we are poor spiritless ignorant peasants, who were born to toil for our betters. But the peasants are beginning to open their eyes and to feel their strength — too long have they been hoodwinked by Baal's priests — by hired and tampered with preachers, wolves in sheep's clothing, who take the wages of sin, and do the work of iniquity, "each one looking to his gain in his quarter."

CANADIANS! Do you love freedom? I know you do. Do you hate oppression? Who dare deny it? Do you wish perpetual peace, and a government founded upon the eternal heaven-born principle of the Lord Jesus Christ — a government bound to enforce the law to do to each other as you would be done by? Then buckle on your armour, and put down the villains who oppress and enslave our country — put them down in the name of that God who goes forth with the armies of his people, and whose bible shows us that it is by the same human means whereby you put to death thieves and murderers, and imprison and banish wicked individuals, that you must put down, in the strength of the Almighty, those governments which, like these bad individuals, trample on the law, and destroy its usefulness. You give a bounty for wolves' scalps. Why? Because wolves harass you. The bounty you must pay for freedom (blessed word) is to give the strength of your arms to put down tyranny at Toronto. One short hour will deliver our country from the oppressor; and freedom in religion, peace and tranquillity, equal laws and an improved country will be the prize. We contend, that in all laws made, or to be made, every person shall be bound alike — neither should any tenure, estate, charter, degree, birth or place, confer any exemption from the ordinary course of legal proceedings and responsibilities whereunto others are subjected.

CANADIANS! God has shown that he is with our brethren, for he has given them the encouragement of success. Captains, Colonels, Volunteers, Artillerymen, Privates, the base, the vile hirelings of our unlawful oppressors have already bit the dust in hundreds in Lower Canada; and although the Roman Catholic and Episcopal Bishops and Archdeacons, are bribed by large sums of money to instruct their flocks that they should be obedient to a government which defies the law, and is therefore unlawful, and ought to be put down, yet God has opened the eyes of the people to the wickedness of these reverent sinners, so that they hold them in derision, just as god's prophet Elijah did the priests of Baal of old and their sacrifices. Is there any one afraid to go to fight for freedom, let him remember, that

God sees with equal eye, as Lord of all,
A Hero perish, or a Sparrow fall.

That power that protected ourselves and our forefathers in the deserts of Canada — that preserved from the cholera those whom He would — that brought us safely to this continent through the dangers of the Atlantic waves — aye, and who watched over us from infancy to manhood, will be in the midst of us in the day of our struggle for our liberties, and for Governors of our free choice, who would not dare to trample on the laws they had sworn to maintain. In the present struggle, we may be sure, that if we do not rise and put down Head and his lawless myrmidons, they will gather all the rogues and villains in the Country together — arm them — and then deliver our farms, our families, and our country to their brutality — to that it has come, we must put them down, or they will utterly destroy this country. If we move now, as one man, to crush the tyrant's power, to establish free institutions founded on God's law, we will prosper, for He who commands the winds and waves will be with us — but if we are cowardly and mean-spirited, a woeful and a dark day is surely before us.

CANADIANS! The struggle will be of short duration in Lower Canada, for the people are united as one man. Out of Montreal and Quebec, they are as 100 to 1 — here reformers are as 10 to 1 — and if we rise with one consent to overthrow despotism, we will make quick work of it.

Mark all those who join our enemies — act as spies for them — fight for them — or aid them — these men's properties shall pay the expense of the struggle — they are traitors to Canadian Freedom, and as such we will deal with them.

CANADIANS! It is the design of the Friends of Liberty to give several hundred acres to every Volunteer — to root up the unlawful Canada Company, and give free deeds to all settlers who live on their lands — to give free gifts of the Clergy Reserve lots, to good citizens who have settled on them — and the like to settlers on Church of England Glebe Lots, so that the yeomanry may feel independent, and be able to improve the country, instead of sending the fruit of their labour to foreign lands. The fifty-seven Rectories will be at once given to the people, and all public lands used for Education, Internal Improvements, and the public good. £100,000 pounds drawn from us in payment of the salaries of bad men in office, will be reduced to one quarter, or much less, and the remainder will go to improve bad roads and to "make crooked paths straight," law will be ten times more cheap and easy — the bickerings of priests will cease with the funds that keep them up — and men of wealth and prop-erty from other lands will soon raise our farms to four times their present value. We have given Head and his employers a trial of forty-five years — five years longer than the Israelites were detained in the wilderness. The promised land is now before us — up then and take it — but set not the torch to one house in Toronto, unless we are fired at from the houses, in which case self-preservation will teach us to put down those who would murder us when up in the defence of the laws. There are some rich men now, as there were in Christ's time, who would go with us in prosperity, but who will skulk in the rear, because of their large possessions — mark them! They are those who in after years will seek to corrupt our people, and change free institutions into an aristocracy of wealth, to grind the poor, and make laws to fetter their energies.

MARK MY WORDS, CANADIANS!

The struggle is begun — it might end in freedom — but timidity, cowardice, or tampering on our part will only delay its close. We cannot be reconciled to Britain — we have humbled ourselves to the Pharaoh of England, to the Ministers, and great people, and they will neither rule us justly nor let us go — we are determined never to rest until independence is ours — the prize is a splendid one. A country larger than France or England; natural resources equal to our most boundless wishes — a government of equal laws — religion pure and undefiled — perpetual peace — education to all — free trade with all the world — but stop — I never could enumerate all the blessings attendant on independence!

Up then, brave Canadians! Get ready your rifles, and make short work of it; a connection with England would involve us in all her wars, undertaken for her own advantage, never for ours; with governors from England, we will have bribery at elections, corruption, villainy and perpetual discord in every township, but Independence would give us the means of enjoying many blessings. Our enemies in Toronto are in terror and dismay — they know their wickedness and dread our vengeance. Fourteen armed men were sent out at the dead hour of night by the traitor Gurnett to drag on a felon's cell, the sons of our worthy and noble minded brother departed, Joseph Sheppard, on a simple and frivolous charge of trespass, brought by a Tory fool; and though it ended in smoke, it showed too evidently Head's feelings. Is there to be an end of these things? Aye, and now's the day and the hour! Woe be to those who oppose us, for "In God is our trust."

The rebellion began a week after the broadsheet appeared. It started in confusion, perhaps because the leadership had not been clearly defined, perhaps because of optimism, perhaps because of poor organization, or perhaps because Mackenzie was not entirely capable of agreeing to appropriate strategy or giving voice to it.

The plan was that the march on Toronto — the destination was the lieutenant-governor's house, and possibly City Hall, where the guns were stored — would occur on Thursday, December 7. The rebels were to gather at Montgomery's Tavern on Yonge Street, just north of the current Eglinton Avenue, on the Wednesday. But on Saturday, December 2, John Rolph picked up gossip that Head and his supporters were organizing and planning to arrest rebel leaders but were not yet ready to offer strong resistance. He thought the rebels' advantage lay in striking quickly. Without consulting others, he proposed that the march on the city should occur on Monday, December 4.

Mackenzie was rallying supporters in late November

and early December and was not in the city. Rolph sent a message to him, suggesting the change in date, in care of David Gibson's house on Yonge Street, just north of Sheppard Avenue. (Gibson's 1851 house, built to replace the home that was destroyed in a fire set by government supporters after the rebellion, still stands.) That message reached Gibson on Saturday and since Mackenzie was not there, Gibson forwarded it to Samuel Lount's home, further north at Holland Landing. But Mackenzie got Rolph's message only when he arrived at Gibson's home late on Sunday. In fact, many others had heard the suggestion, which was almost general knowledge, and some rebels, assuming the date had been changed, began travelling on Monday morning to the rendezvous point. Mackenzie had to make his way to Montgomery's Tavern.

The scene there on Monday was one of disorganization. The rebel leaders had not made a real plan, and their supporters, who trickled in all day, had not been formed into a fighting unit. No one was ready to march on the city. No arrangements had been made for provisioning, and there was difficulty finding food for the men who had gathered. It was decided to delay the attack on the city until Tuesday morning. Rolph travelled north from the city for a meeting with Mackenzie at Gibson's home, bringing the news that the French-Canadian rebels had been badly defeated and recommending that the uprising be abandoned. It was too late at this point to stop the course of events. Rolph returned to the city.

The gathering of several hundred rebels at Montgomery's did not go unnoticed. Colonel Robert Moodie, a veteran of the War of 1812 who lived close by the tavern, noted the large assembly of people and decided to ride into the city to warn the lieutenant-governor and his supporters.

The rebels had posted guards south on Yonge Street. When Moodie tried to ride through the roadblock, there was an exchange of gunfire and he was severely wounded. He was taken to Montgomery's Tavern, where he died several hours later, apparently in great pain.

Meanwhile Mackenzie and several others set out from Montgomery's to reconnoitre, going farther down Yonge Street. They came upon two government loyalists, Alderman John Powell and Archibald Macdonald, and they took them as prisoners. Mackenzie asked if they were armed, they said they weren't, and Mackenzie took them at their word without making a careful search. (Later Powell claimed he had never been asked if he was armed.) A few minutes later, Powell produced a pistol and shot and killed Mackenzie's colleague Anthony Anderson, one of the few rebels knowledgeable of military tactics. Powell escaped, making his way back to Toronto, where he warned the lieutenant-governor of the rebel uprising. Immediately the bells of many of the city's churches were set ringing to warn the population. Mackenzie returned to Montgomery's Tavern.

On Tuesday morning, December 5, there was continued perplexity as to what exactly should be done, undoubtedly caused by the suggestion that the uprising be moved forward three days. The military man expected to lead the rebels, Colonel Anthony Van Egmond, a veteran of the Napoleonic Wars and a Reform candidate in the 1836 election, was still travelling from Huron County with plans of arriving on Thursday, as previously agreed. Mackenzie was reported to be in a very agitated state. It was decided that the rebels would march south, dividing into two groups, one under the leadership of Lount, one under Mackenzie.

On the government side, Sir Francis Bond Head had decided to make an offer of a truce. He appointed two men to present this offer, Robert Baldwin and John Rolph. Rolph was obviously in a quandary, since refusing Head's offer to be a mediator would be a clear indication that he sided with the rebels. Almost always an opportunist in his long political life, he agreed to be Head's agent. Preceded by a white flag, Rolph and Baldwin came up Yonge Street at midday as the rebels headed south. They met just south of St. Clair Avenue, at Gallows Hill. There was surprise among the rebels that Rolph was an emissary for Head. Baldwin and Rolph offered amnesty in return for dispersal. Mackenzie and the rebels agreed to this proposal on condition that a convention would be held to discuss the policies of the province, and that the agreement would be reduced to writing. Rolph and Baldwin undertook to get Head's assent.

The two sides withdrew. Many rebels wondered about Rolph — wasn't he on the rebel side? — and they had doubts about a continued march on the city. For his part,

Mackenzie was still flustered, and some worried about his sanity. He wore several overcoats, claiming they would protect him from musket fire. Rolph and Baldwin learned, on returning to the city, that Head had no intention of having further communication with the rebels — he probably had now been fully briefed about their chaotic state. The two men rode back north and gave Mackenzie the bad news. But Rolph apparently made an aside to Mackenzie that he should come into the city as quickly as possible.

Later in the afternoon, Mackenzie and a few colleagues travelled down Yonge Street and set fire to the house of a Dr. Horne, manager of the Bank of Upper Canada, claiming that the building was full of spies. It was an act that had no strategic importance for the rebels. Lount persuaded Mackenzie not to burn down a second house.

In the evening, Mackenzie and Lount led a group of more than five hundred men down Yonge Street. It promised to be a serious assault on the city. Near the present College Street (well south of the toll bar at Bloor Street) the rebels met Sheriff Jarvis and a group of government loyalists. Shooting began, some men fell to the ground — and both sides were confronted with the terrifying possibility of fatal consequences. Everyone retreated in fear and disarray. Several rebels had been wounded and one killed. The lack of discipline and leadership on the rebel side was apparent, and in spite of Mackenzie's strong efforts to keep his group pushing forward, the surprised rebels pulled back and dispersed. They scattered up Yonge Street and back to Montgomery's Tavern, when in fact the city was theirs for the taking, since Jarvis's small group of defenders had also scattered.

On Wednesday, December 6, the forces at Montgomery's remained in a muddle. Peter Matthews arrived with a group of sixty men, swelling rebel numbers at Montgomery's to more than five hundred, but Mackenzie and Lount were unable to rally them to action. They planned a raid on the city for the next day, December 7, when Van Egmond would join them.

Mackenzie travelled west and intercepted government mail as it passed the Peacock Tavern at Keele and Davenport Streets, in the wild hope of learning government intentions. It is unclear whether robbery was a part of his interception. In the city, Head consolidated his troops, which numbered close to fifteen hundred men. Before the close of day, Rolph had left the city, seeking safety in the United States.

When Van Egmond arrived at Montgomery's on Thursday, he counselled immediate dispersal as the situation seemed hopeless. Mackenzie refused this course of action. The debate about strategy was interrupted by news of the approach of a much larger number of government forces — about eleven hundred men — under the leadership of James Fitzgibbon and Allan MacNab. Van Egmond led his men down Yonge. There was a brief exchange of gunfire between the two forces on the rise of land south of Eglinton Avenue. The rebels quickly fled. Head's forces continued north and burned down Montgomery's Tavern. One rebel, Ludwig Wideman, was killed and several others died later of wounds. There were no government casualties.

Head immediately issued a proclamation offering a reward for the capture of the rebel leaders.

To the Queen's Faithful Subjects in Upper Canada

In a time of profound peace, while every one was quietly following his occupations, feeling secure under the protection of Laws, a band of rebels, instigated by a few malignant and disloyal men, has had the wickedness and audacity to assemble with Arms, and to attack and Murder the Queen's Subjects on the Highway — to Burn and Destroy their property — to Rob the Public Mails — and to threaten to Plunder the Banks — and to Fire the City of Toronto.

Brave and Loyal People of Upper Canada, we have been long suffering from the acts and endeavours of concealed Traitors, but this is the first time that the Rebellion has dared to shew itself openly in the land, in the absence of invasion by any Foreign Enemy.

Let every man do his duty now, and it will be the last time that we or our children shall see our lives or properties endangered, or the Authority of our Gracious Queen insulted by such treacherous and ungrateful men....

Be vigilant, patient and active — leave punishment to the Laws — our first object is to arrest all those who have been guilty of Rebellion, Murder and Robbery — And to aid us in this, a Reward is hereby offered of

ONE THOUSAND POUNDS,

to any one who will apprehend, and deliver up to justice, WILLIAM LYON MACKENZIE; and FIVE HUNDRED POUNDS to any one who will apprehend and deliver up to justice, DAVID GIBSON — or SAMUEL LOUNT — or JESSE LLOYD — or SILAS FLETCHER — and the same reward and a free pardon will be given to any of those accomplices who will render this public service, except he or they shall have committed, in his own person, the crime of Murder or Arson.

And all, but the Leaders above named, who have been seduced to join in this unnatural Rebellion, are hereby called to return to their duty to their Sovereign — to obey the Laws — and to live henceforth as good and faithful Subjects — and they will find the Government of their Queen as indulgent as it is just.

GOD SAVE THE QUEEN.

Thursday 3 o'clock, P.M. 7th Dec.

The Party of Rebels, under their Chief Leaders, is wholly dispersed, and flying before the Loyal Militia. The only thing that remains to be done, is to find them, and arrest them.

Mackenzie made a remarkable escape alone over several days to the Niagara frontier, being hidden along the way by an extraordinarily supportive rural population who provided food, lodging, and good hideouts. "I had risked much for Canadians," Mackenzie later wrote of his

escape, "and served them long, and as faithfully as I could
— and now, when a fugitive, I found them ready to risk
life and property to aid me — far more ready to risk the
dungeon, by harbouring me, than to accept Sir Francis
Head's thousand pounds." He reached Buffalo on
December 11. Over the next ten days, the ineffective rebel
force under Charles Duncombe was broken in Brantford,
Ingersoll, London, and other points west.

Many of Mackenzie's colleagues were not so lucky.
Lount was captured after an unsuccessful attempt to row
across Lake Erie: he was blown to the Canadian shore
and captured, a farmer claiming the reward. Van Egmond
was arrested and died in his cell in the King Street jail on
December 30 from the cold and the damp. More than
eight hundred men were arrested.

Trials were held in Toronto in March 1838, a few
weeks later in Hamilton, and in early May in London.
Although the colonial secretary, Lord Glenelg, had
advised against executions, two men were hanged for
participating in the rebellion. Peter Matthews and Samuel
Lount pleaded guilty, and the heartfelt calls that their lives
be spared fell on deaf ears: they both were hanged behind
the courthouse just east of the present-day Toronto Street.
A broken pillar marks their resting place in the
Necropolis, the same graveyard where Mackenzie is
buried. Many of those arrested were acquitted, found
their charges dismissed, or were pardoned. Seven men
were sentenced to transportation to Australia, but when
their ship reached England, a lawyer made arguments

resulting in their release. Head was succeeded as lieutenant-governor by Sir George Arthur, the vicious governor of Van Diemen's Land (now Tasmania), Australia.

Skirmishes continued between the rebels and the government over the next twelve months in other parts of Upper Canada. Mackenzie would spend more than a decade in exile.

9 · Exile and Decline

TWELVE YEARS OF EXILE were personally costly to Mackenzie, and his return would present a diminished man, still able to stand up for public values but without the drive for change or the instinct for the telling phrase or action. His final decade of life in Upper Canada was anticlimactic compared with the intensity of the seventeen years between his arrival in Canada and the rebellion.

After he arrived in Buffalo on December 11, 1837, Mackenzie's main interest was in continuing the rebellion. With several dozen men he occupied Navy Island on the American side of the Niagara River and declared a provisional government. The proclamation listed Mackenzie as "Chairman pro tem," and named the members of the provisional government as Nelson Gorham, Adam Graham, Samuel Lount, John Hawk, Silas Fletcher, Jacob Rymall, Jesse Lloyd, William Doyle, Thomas Darling, A. Van Egmond, and Charles Duncombe, even though several were not present — Lount and Van Egmond had been arrested, and Duncombe was still battling in western Upper Canada. The proclamation owes much to the *Seventh Report of the Grievances Committee*, with the familiar list of needed reforms. Also included is the suggestion of a canal system linking Lake Superior and the other great lakes to the St. Lawrence River and the ocean.

It was a brave document, issued in the face of defeat. Sir Francis Bond Head fairly gloated at the outcome and counted himself victorious over that demon "democracy." Early in 1838 Head ruminated on his accomplishments, and recounted in a report to British authorities the task he thought was expected of him during his brief official tenure in Upper Canada, using language that now seems unnecessarily provocative. He wrote boldly, "That I was sentenced to contend on the soil of America with Democracy, and that if I did not overpower it, it would overpower me, were solemn facts, which for some weeks had been perfectly evident to my mind; but by far the most difficult problem I had to solve was, *where* I ought to make my stand." He explained in a convoluted fashion how he saved the colonies from the nonsense of equality.

Whatever may be the opinion of the public on this subject, I shall always believe that, had I, inexperienced and unsupported, fallen as soon as I reached my post, his Majesty's Government would have been liable to impeachment for the loss of our North American colonies. Nevertheless, I really do them the justice to believe that they were so intoxicated by the insane theory of conciliating democracy, that they actually believed the people of Upper Canada would throw up their hats and be delighted at the vulgarity of seeing the representative of their sovereign arrive among them as an actor of all work, without dignity of station, demeanour, or conduct: in short, like a republican governor, who, from his cradle, has been brought up to reckon "that all men are born equal" — that the fabric of human society has neither top nor bottom — that the protection of property of all description belongs to the multitude — and that the will of the mob is the real "law of the land."

Head understood and played on the significant tension in the body politic — obviously fair game for exploitation now that Mackenzie was exiled to American soil — that those advocating American-style reforms were probably secretly disloyal to the British Crown. He was clear about the contrast: "So long as in the United States democracy displayed only its brilliant flowers, considerable danger existed of the weed being rashly transplanted into this neighbouring soil; but since the poisonous properties of its fruit have become known to us, the attachment of the Upper Canadians to their British constitution has, from deliberate conviction, gradually become what I have described it to be. I firmly believe that this good feeling will increase — that the disease of democracy has ceased to be infectious — that we have now nothing to dread but its contagion, and, consequently, nothing to avoid but its actual contact." He concluded his report with the good news:

I have no hesitation whatever in declaring to your Lordship, that upon the loyalty of the people of Upper Canada his Majesty's Government may now build as a rock. I declare to your Lordship that in England there does not exist a more sensible attachment to the British constitution, and to the person of our Sovereign, than here. The owners of property in Upper Canada dislike democracy: they dislike it infinitely more than people in England do, because there it is a fine omne-ignorum pro-magnifico theory, that no man understands — whereas *here*, it is seen practically working before our eyes in the United States; and it is because the British population in Upper Canada see it in operation, that they deliberately detest it, in which feeling, or rather judgment, they are joined by many of the Americans themselves, who sorrowfully foresee that Lynch law must ere long unavoidably treat their rights, their hard-earned property, and their religion, just as the cataract of Niagara everlastingly behaves to the calm, gliding waters of Lake Erie.

It was a fine image Head offered: democracy crashing to defeat over Niagara Falls. Language about democracy was not in common use at this time. One writer notes, "The word Democracy ... was understood to mean something vaguely terrible which might come, and would come if the respectable classes did not stand together," and continues to elucidate how Head would have regarded the idea: "If Democracy came, kings and Lords would disappear and old landmarks of every description would be swept away. Nothing could resist the flood of popular domination if the dykes of patronage and borough mongering were once removed. The "people" were pictured as a horde of ragamuffins howling for the ballot and the blood of the aristocracy."

In exile, Mackenzie applied the "democracy" word to himself, writing, "My creed has been social democracy — or equality of each man before society — and political democracy, or the equality of each man before the law."

But the rebellious instinct was generally spent. In early January, President Martin Van Buren warned that rebel rumblings on American soil could be interpreted as breaches of the Neutrality Act, and on January 4, Mackenzie left Navy Island with his wife, who had joined him two weeks earlier. Returning to Buffalo, he was indeed arrested under the Neutrality Act, and was released on bail posted by supporters. As Mackenzie moved around northern New York State, rebel attacks were launched across the border, but Mackenzie played no part in planning or executing them. In March 1838, he arrived in New York

City, where he found lodgings with a friend and fellow printer; his mother and the rest of the children came a few months later. In May he began publishing *Mackenzie's Weekly Gazette*, which chewed over the facts of the rebellion and once again set out an agenda for Canada. But a Canadian audience was hard to reach since this paper was denied entry into Canada. Mackenzie's financial position was weak. In considerable despair, it seems he decided to apply for American citizenship, but the impulse passed.

He toured Philadelphia and Washington late in 1838, giving speeches along the way, then headed north to the frontier — where there had been sporadic forays onto Canadian soil by rebel supporters — to investigate the depth of the support. The picture was not encouraging. The last issue of the *Weekly Gazette* was published in New York in January 1839, shortly before the birth of the Mackenzies' eleventh child, named William Lyon Mackenzie. The family relocated to Rochester, where a new *Gazette* was launched in February. There Mackenzie linked up with his old friend John Montgomery, whose tavern had been the launching pad for the events in early December. The two started an organization favouring Canadian independence, but it was never strong. Money was a continuing worry. Mackenzie had no steady source of income.

In mid-June his trial for breach of the Neutrality Act began. He did not have a lawyer but defended himself, a difficult position given the publication of his proclamation of a provisional government. It was not his finest hour.

One historian wrote, "The trial illustrates some of Mackenzie's most unfortunate failings: his verbosity, his inconsistencies, his over-confidence in his own abilities, his tendency to incriminate others and to find excuses for his own failings." Mackenzie was convicted on June 21 and sentenced to eighteen months in jail in Rochester. While he was in jail, his ninety-year-old mother fell deathly ill. John Montgomery arranged to lay a charge against a boarder and called Mackenzie as a witness. The trial was held in Montgomery's premises, and Mackenzie was brought there to testify. The judge turned a blind eye to this device that permitted Mackenzie to say a last good-bye to his mother, who was dying in an upstairs room in the establishment. She passed away on December 22, 1839.

In October a shot was fired through the small window of Mackenzie's cell, but he was not injured, and in spite of his claim that the event was politically motivated, it was impossible to prove what the incident was about. Many petitioned for his release — three hundred thousand by one count — and finally, on May 10, 1840, President Van Buren remitted the sentence and Mackenzie was freed.

But exile is a poor kind of freedom. Mackenzie was penniless and disillusioned, relying on friends to support his family. He began another newspaper, the *Volunteer*, voicing the same concerns as the *Gazette* (which he had continued to publish in jail), and it lasted for but a few sporadic issues during 1841 and 1842. He knew of the significant changes proposed by Lord Durham for Canada but was powerless to affect them. Lord Durham had been sent by colonial authorities to report on the aftermath of the rebellion, and in mid-1839 he recommended that the Executive Council be chosen by the assembly. Next year came his proposal for the union of Upper and Lower Canada, which was quickly implemented. Mackenzie chafed at the former change as being ineffective, and complained that the latter was a poor substitute for giving independence to the provinces. But his opinion mattered little: he was in exile.

In mid-1842 he again moved with his family to New York City, where he found work as the actuary and librarian of the Mechanics' Institute, a form of lending library. His thirteenth and last child, Isabel Grace, was born in February 1843. (Her son William Lyon Mackenzie King was the well-known descendant of Mackenzie who became Canadian prime minister in the first half of the twentieth century.) A few months later Mackenzie received American citizenship. But he remained impecunious. His salary came from fees he was to collect, and they were meagre. He held the position until October 1843, when he resigned and started another newspaper, the *Examiner*. It published rather scurrilous information about Martin Van Buren, who before he was elected president in 1836 had been a New York senator with approval powers over bank charters. This paper, too, had a short life, surviving but three issues.

In 1844 he achieved a small appointment in the archives of the Customs House. There he gained access to private letters which were the basis of his pamphlet "Lives and Opinions of Benjamin Franklin Butler and Jesse Hoyt." Hoyt was a Van Buren appointee, and the pamphlet set out letters which created a solid case of financial intrigue involving Van Buren during his days as senator. Mackenzie once again realized that his hope did not lie in American democratic practice, which had its own foibles and corruptions. It was a popular pamphlet — fifty thousand copies were printed — and was followed in 1846 by *The Life and Times of Martin Van Buren*, a book which largely reprinted the same documents as the pamphlet, with additions. This was more a collection of letters than a book. Neither publication was of financial benefit to Mackenzie.

In 1846 he was retained by the *New York Tribune* to report on the New York State Constitutional Convention in Albany. He moved to Albany for six months, filing daily reports on the discussions of all the issues he most cared about: court reform, banking, education, municipal reform. The convention ended in November, and Mackenzie was again without work and without funds. He picked up small writing assignments and returned to New York in April 1847. It was almost a hand-to-mouth existence for Mackenzie and his family. Barbara was put in the Bloomindale Asylum for the Insane in March 1848, causing great distress to Mackenzie. She remained there for three months. In June twelve-year-old Margaret died. "O, but she was a noble creature," wrote Mackenzie, "and how sorrow[ful] I am that I did not do more for her — and that my wayward fate entailed on her such a load of early woes!"

In January 1849, the Canadian government passed a general amnesty bill which allowed his return; previous bills seemed to have been designed to allow anyone but Mackenzie re-entry to Canada. With his ten-year-old son, William, he set out for Montreal, arriving on February 25.

The timing of his return was inauspicious. The Rebellion Losses Bill was being debated in the Assembly of the United Provinces, meeting in Montreal. The bill proposed to compensate Lower Canadians for property damaged in the rebellion (as had been done in Upper Canada), which set Tories aflame since they interpreted the bill as support for those who were disloyal. The result was considerable unrest. Arriving at the library of the Assembly in Montreal, Mackenzie was recognized by an Upper Canadian Tory and unceremoniously hounded from the building. In Kingston, where he stayed with his brother-in-law George Baxter, he was burned in effigy. A week later, in Toronto, a melee occurred in front of the house where he was staying, and again he was burned in effigy. Much glass was broken, although none of the rioters were arrested. He went back to New York. He visited Canada for four weeks later in the year without incident; and putting his family up again with the Baxters in Kingston, he made his way to Toronto in June 1850, where he rented a house on Yonge Street at the corner of Alice (now Dundas) Street. His family joined him within a few weeks.

Toronto had changed since the Rebellion of 1837. It

was now a bustling metropolis of thirty thousand inhabi-
tants — three times as large as when Mackenzie had fled.
A fire had devastated the buildings on King Street, and
new buildings were underway: St. Lawrence Hall at Jarvis
Street, a grand new structure for St. James' Cathedral at
Church Street. City Hall had moved to the building at the
southwest corner of Jarvis and Front Streets, where it
stayed for almost fifty years. A new jail designed by John
Howard had been constructed near the site of the former
Parliament Buildings on the south side of Front Street, and
Howard's impressive Mental Asylum for the mentally ill
was completed west along Queen Street, at Ossington.
Little Trinity Church had been built on King Street, and
the Church of the Holy Trinity now stood north of Queen
between Yonge and Bay. Charles Dickens had visited the
city in the previous decade and noticed "the wild and
rabid Toryism of Toronto," but that had probably passed
with the influx of immigrants. George Brown had founded
the reform newspaper the *Globe* in 1844, and it was very
successful. A telegraph now linked Toronto to Montreal
and New York City. There were fifteen public schools.
The Clergy Reserves system was largely being disman-
tled. Much more land was under development in the
province, and trains and steam engines were about to
enter the city.

　　More important, the political climate had changed. The
rebellion had convinced British authorities that something
must be done — hence Lord Durham's visit and report.
Union with Lower Canada had been in place since 1841,

and the Executive Council was now responsible to the
assembly rather than to the representative of the British
crown. The Family Compact was no longer a useful whip-
ping boy.

To resolve his money troubles, Mackenzie applied to
collect past debts incurred in his work on the Welland
Canal committee before the rebellion (in this endeavour
he met with some success) and compensation for the
pillaging of his home and his press after the rebellion.
Then, in February 1851, the Assembly member for the
Haldimand riding (on the north shore of Lake Erie) died.
Mackenzie offered himself as a candidate in the by-
election.

Times had changed since he had first run for office in
1828. A political party tagged the "Clear Grits" had
emerged to promote his ideas in a strange mixture —
agrarian republicanism, free trade, election of judges and
other state institutions — and they felt he should be their
candidate or not run at all. But Mackenzie was his own
man, and his intrusion meant that voters were presented
with a number of progressive choices. George Brown,
editor of the *Globe*, was a Reform candidate in support of
the Baldwin-LaFontaine government, which stood for
responsible government but (in the opinion of some) sub-
verted the interests of Upper Canada to Lower Canada,
where Louis-Hippolyte LaFontaine had his political base.
Other candidates were A.N. Case, running as a Reformer
(he lived in the riding), and Ronald McKinnon, a local
Tory businessman. Mackenzie emerged the victor with

294 of almost 800 votes cast. McKinnon came second with 266 votes; it appeared that he was elected to the second seat on his past record of opposition to the Reform-dominated government.

In spite of the changed political climate, Mackenzie picked up where he left off: he opposed the government of the day. He continued to advocate punishing banks rather than enabling them, reform of the court system, abolition of imprisonment for debt, and opposition to railway requests for debt guarantees. Government members found it irritating to listen to his long speeches and his demands for recorded votes. There was a sense that his time had passed. The fact that he was an independent when political parties were on the ascendant limited his effectiveness.

But when a general election was held in December 1851, he was handily re-elected. Membership in the Assembly carried small compensation that did nothing to alleviate Mackenzie's poverty. The legislature met in Quebec, requiring his presence there for much of the year, with his family living in Toronto. That did not make things easier for him. He did some writing for the *Toronto Examiner*, published by his friend James Lesslie, but had a falling-out when Lesslie refused to publish a letter that he felt was damaging to the Reform cause. Mackenzie followed his familiar course, starting another publication, *Mackenzie's Weekly Message*, in December 1852. After the assembly adjourned the following June, he had little news to print and instead regurgitated stories about the rebellion.

Parliament was prorogued in June 1853, an election
was held that summer, and Mackenzie was narrowly
re-elected in Haldimand. His poverty continued, as did his
lack of influence. He dropped his own publication and
resumed writing for the *Examiner*, but when it was unex-
pectedly sold to Brown's *Globe* in August 1855, he restarted
his own paper once again. Brown's paper was very successful; Mackenzie's was marginal in every sense.

The year 1855 offered promise for Mackenzie as interest in the state of the union of Upper and Lower Canada
grew. Mackenzie opposed union and spoke openly against
it, sometimes provoking hostility. Brown hoped that "rep
by pop" — representation by population — would give
Upper Canada the clout needed for more self-government
and freedom from Lower Canada's control, but Mackenzie
thought rep by pop didn't go far enough. Mackenzie criticized union in a *Reader's Almanac* that he published in
April 1856, noting that Upper Canada was largely English-
speaking and Protestant while Lower Canada was largely
French speaking and Roman Catholic. He thought this
required two distinct court systems, two distinct education systems, and no fixed location for the government;
and he feared that Upper Canada, the wealthier of the
two partners, would be stuck with a portion of Lower
Canada's debts as well as its own.

In late 1856, Brown created the Reform Alliance to
support his cause, but Mackenzie was not invited to the
group's meetings. One politician called him "a person of
no influence." Mackenzie's decline must have been obvi-

ous. James Lesslie began a campaign to collect funds to provide a Toronto homestead for Mackenzie and his family. In his poverty, Mackenzie argued that the funds would be better disbursed directly to him, but it was another argument he did not win.

In the election in late 1857, Mackenzie garnered 38 per cent of the vote in Haldimand, in a close race with two other candidates, and was narrowly re-elected. In this election, he expressed support for Brown in opposition to the unionist politics of John A. Macdonald. The election gave Mackenzie a seat in Parliament but he had little useful to say, and he resigned in bitterness in August 1858. He continued the sporadic publication of the *Message* until the end of the year, and it was revived for an issue or two more in the next few years.

He seemed sadly confused. He thought of going to Dundee and went as far as New York but, penniless, returned to Toronto. As Brown convened a meeting in opposition to the union of Upper and Lower Canada, Mackenzie raised a weak voice to urge annexation to the United States.

By early 1859, more than seven thousand dollars had been collected by Lesslie for a Mackenzie home, and a house was purchased at 117 Bond Street, which the Mackenzies occupied in October. A month later the bodies of his rebel colleagues Peter Matthews and Samuel Lount were exhumed and reburied in the Toronto Necropolis. In February his daughter Barbara died in the Provincial Mental Asylum. Mackenzie remained poor, his health slowly declined, and he died peacefully on August 28, 1861. Wrote George Brown the next day in the *Globe*, "No history of Canada can be complete in which his name does not occupy a conspicuous, and we must add notwithstanding his errors, an honourable position. Whatever may have been the means employed, his aims were honest and public spirited. He was no money hunter, he was the friend of purity and economy in the administration of public affairs." His funeral cortege stretched for half a mile behind the hearse taking his body to be buried in the Necropolis.

10 · Mackenzie's Political Ideas in Today's World

MACKENZIE SEEMS TO have disappointed many commentators by his apparent inability to express a cogent philosophy of his politics. They have looked in vain for the telling phrase which might sit beside the axioms of other political philosophers of the nineteenth century such as John Stuart Mill or Karl Marx. Perhaps they have been looking in the wrong place. Mackenzie prized debate and action, and instead of worrying about a detectable philosophical underpinning, concerned himself with the actions which distinguished the kind of political leader he wished to be rather than with theories of the democratic state.

Thus his ideas seem workaday, not particularly exalted. But they turn out to be crucial to the practice of responsive, responsible government in both his time and ours. Upon distilling Mackenzie's plethora of words and actions and the comments of contemporaries, essayists, and historians, one can discover his principles without much difficulty, once one remembers that he was more concerned with doing the right thing than thinking the right thoughts. The task he set himself, at a time when the idea of elite decision-making was under attack, was to outline a course of action that gave value to ordinary people. This chapter defines the parameters of those actions and suggests how those notions are being interpreted in our time.

Mackenzie often referred to the actions he considered important to his style of political involvement, but he never set them out in a clear manner. By interpreting them according to today's political behaviour, one begins to understand the depth of his analysis of what has come to be known as the "democratic process." The principles drawn from his work are set out below, followed by commentary on the current situation in Upper Canada, now Ontario.

The public is entitled to full information concerning the issues and the conduct of public business.

In Mackenzie's day this was a relatively new idea, and it sprang from his belief that ordinary people had a legitimate place in public decision-making. He believed passionately in this simple idea, and it lay at the foundation of his work as a publisher. The importance of information being public became relatively well established in the mid-twentieth century, but it has since declined substantially. In the new century the public is routinely denied basic information about government activities, and governments often go to extraordinary lengths to keep their actions out of the public eye.

The practice in Ontario during the 1970s and 1980s of explaining legislative intentions in laymen's language through a White Paper and then, when the bill was introduced, providing an explanatory text of the legislation itself has been abandoned. Legislative proposals are kept private within the senior circles of the government until first reading of the bill, when they are sprung on a public surprised often by both the subject matter and the proposed course of action. The legal text is usually obscure and complicated, even to a lawyer, but it is not explained. What used to be a leisurely process of three readings with public hearings has been collapsed into a rush of several weeks with little or no opportunity provided for public hearings or public discussion. In at least one case in the past few years the Ontario government attempted to begin second reading of the bill — which is when substantive debate occurs — without providing a copy of the bill to members of the opposition in the legislature. The effect of these changes (one assumes it is also the intention) is to make it difficult for the public to learn about legislation, rather than to help citizens understand it and participate

in debate about the appropriateness of current laws or the
need for new ones.

The bulk of government business involves not new
laws but policies and regulations that by definition are
much less public, and there are many instances of the
government actively attempting to hide this kind of information. For example, on May 4, four weeks before the
1999 provincial election, the government responded to
fears of water shortages and dry wells in southwestern
Ontario by enacting a new regulation prohibiting further
groundwater extraction by large companies. Six months
later, it was learned that a mere two weeks after the election, the government had granted new permits for water
extraction to companies in areas where groundwater
depletion was most worrisome but had said nothing publicly about the breach of the moratorium. "We weren't
hiding it from anyone," a government official said in
November. Perhaps not, but they weren't forthright about
it either. A public haystack is a very large place to secrete
a small amount of information that no one knew they
should be looking for, information that the beneficiary of
the change had no wish to reveal.

Creative use of freedom of information legislation has
also kept information out of public hands. In 1997, the City
of Toronto wanted to obtain a report prepared by provincial staff on the impact of new property tax legislation
proposed by the Ontario government. The report allegedly
showed that the proposed legislation was very damaging
to city homeowners. Unable to obtain it from staff, the city

sought a court order under the Freedom of Information and Protection of Privacy Act to secure the document. The report was placed by provincial officials on a cabinet meeting agenda, and since freedom of information does not extend to cabinet documents, the report was effectively removed from the public domain. The oath of cabinet secrecy was used not to improve decision-making but to deny information to the public.

For those who would use a shareholder analogy to describe the relationship between the cabinet and the citizens, such behaviour would be deemed illegal. "Information is a valuable commodity," a former commissioner of the Ontario Securities Commission wrote in the *Globe and Mail*. "It is, and should be regarded as, a corporate asset held for the benefit of the corporation. Thus the use of material, undisclosed information by insiders and others who are in a special relationship with the corporation is akin to theft." The *Globe and Mail* went on to conclude editorially, "At its core, capitalism depends for its efficiency and credibility, on information broadly and generally shared by all participants in the market." Mackenzie would probably have reworded this statement slightly, given his interests. "At its core," he quite plausibly could have written, "good government depends for its efficiency and credibility, on information broadly and generally shared by all citizens in the country."

Municipal governments operate much more openly than senior governments, given that provincial legislation requires that (except in very limited circumstances)

council meetings must be held in public, ensuring that the
staff reports being considered by the councillors are also
public. But the sensible idea that the public's business
should be done in public has found less and less favour at
the provincial and federal levels. Mackenzie would complain mightily about the provincial and federal practices of
hiding information.

**There must be appropriate opportunities for public
discussion of public issues and the conduct of public
business, and those elected to office have an obligation
to ensure that these opportunities exist.**

Mackenzie encouraged public debate in his writing and in
his actions, and engaged in it with vigour. One looks in
vain over today's political landscape to find such politicians. Many will note that times are different. Television
demands immediate and constant coverage of politicians,
and television news clips can't be left to the chancy out-
comes that typify debates. Every political commentator
can point to the lesson of the 1976 federal election, when
the Conservative leader, Robert Stanfield, indulged in a
game of touch football with colleagues, catching all the
balls he was thrown but one — and the photo of that one
fumble was the news story widely reported. Stanfield was
stuck with the image of a man who fumbles the ball.

Today's leader scripts public appearances carefully to
exclude public events like public debates which may
create embarrassment or force a change in opinion. If

public figures don't encourage public debate and discussion by their own actions, it usually doesn't happen. Yet democracy has little chance to thrive if members of the public do not have the opportunity to create well-formed and informed ideas of what their elected representatives should be doing. This aspect of the political process, which was critical for Mackenzie, is today badly shrivelled.

Interested members of the public will have opportunities to present their opinions to those elected to office.

Mackenzie believed that once people had information and the opportunity to discuss issues with friends and neighbours, they would have reasonable opinions worth expressing to those charged with making a decision. The governing process included setting aside time for people to be heard by those who had been elected to make public decisions.

This process evolved in Ontario for more than a century, giving the public ever more opportunities to speak before legislative committees. But in the last decade of the twentieth century, this practice was terminated by the creative use of the time allocation motion, which sets a date when a bill, after completion of second reading, will return to the legislature for third (and final) reading. In the past, such motions — sometimes called closure — were used to prevent opposition parties from delaying legislation after a full and long debate, but now they are used to prevent public hearings and debate by elected members. This perverse use of time allocation motions grew exponentially after the Mike Harris government was first elected in 1995. They were used four times in the government's first eighteen months but then were quickly applied to all legislative initiatives, so that in the brief thirty-four-day sitting of the Legislative Assembly between October 20 and December 23, 1999, time allocation motions were applied to all eleven government bills introduced, which were all given three readings and royal assent. Public deputations were prohibited on ten bills, and a mere two hours of hearings were permitted on the remaining one.

One impact of this use of the time allocation motion is that elected representatives are denied the opportunity to hear what informed people think of the legislation. Another is that there are no news reports of hearings, which would serve to let members of the wider public learn about government legislation. Apparently this was something the government learned early in 1997 when it permitted several weeks of hearings on the bill which forcibly amalgamated the municipalities in Toronto into one megacity. News reports of the many briefs presented gave the issues wide currency, informing the public and making the bill a matter of public debate. Many people became aware of the impacts of the amalgamation legislation by simply picking up the newspaper or turning on the television, and even though all three Toronto newspapers supported amalgamation editorially, their news pages carried a different story. The news coverage obviously played a large part in the high voter turnout for the referendum on amalgamation in March 1997 and in the astounding 76 per cent vote of opposition.

"There is assuredly no security for good government," Mackenzie said in 1831, "unless both favourable and unfavourable opinions of public men are allowed to be freely circulated." With no hearings, there would have been no coverage and no public debate. In 1997 the government realized it had nothing to gain from a public process, and time allocation became standard practice.

The legislature and its committees need reasonable rules so that elected members are not unduly interrupted by those who want to prevent business from being carried on. But when rules exclude or substantially limit public input, when even elected members are given little opportunity to discuss the legislation, something has gone drastically wrong. It's a return to the dictatorial style of government that Mackenzie found himself up against.

Those elected to office are obliged to listen carefully to what is said by members of the public.

The job of an elected representative in a democracy is often said to be to represent, and there's no more effective way of doing this task than listening. Obviously this cannot be done if there are no opportunities for people to have their say.

In fact, the collapse of representative democracy has been more total in Ontario, since ministers responsible for legislation rarely attend committee meetings to listen to what little debate occurs and seldom participate in debate in the legislature. The nadir of this trend occurred in 1999 with Bill 25, which forcibly amalgamated the many municipalities in Ottawa, Hamilton, and Sudbury into new megacities; arbitrarily reduced the size of Toronto City Council; amended general legislation affecting all municipalities in Ontario; amended various other laws affecting many other municipalities; and permitted cabinet to amend by regulation any laws it felt appropriate in order to implement the bill. (This last provision was perhaps the most dictatorial action taken by a government in Ontario since the Rebellion of 1837: it said the cabinet could make its own laws, without approval of the Assembly. Within six months, and without publicly acknowledging its over-reaching, the government quietly repealed the sections giving the cabinet these extraordinary powers.)

The premier himself promised public hearings on Bill 25 but a time allocation motion prevented that, permitting only two hours and thirty minutes of discussion by elected members on third reading in the assembly. The first hour of that discussion was taken up with speeches by government backbenchers. The minister of municipal affairs, who had introduced the bill, did not speak, nor did any other member of the cabinet. The second hour was allocated to the opposition, the Liberal Party, and only for the last fifteen minutes of this hour did the minister, the premier, and other senior ministers attend the Assembly. They were present for the fifteen minutes allocated to the

New Democratic Party, although throughout his thirty-minute stay the premier chatted with backbenchers in his government, always turning his back to whoever was speaking, making obvious his disdain for the comments of others.

There is little difference between the system in Mackenzie's day, when the elected assembly had no power (power rested in the appointed Legislative and Executive Councils) and the current arrangement, where the public is unable to achieve representation since elected members of the government are shielded from having to listen to the public.

Those elected to office must vote according to their conscience.

Mackenzie's idea of good government relied on an informed public, widespread public debate, direct engagement in public debate by those elected, and active listening. These conditions ensured that elected officials would be in a good position to cast an informed vote. An elected person, he wrote, "looks carefully into the merits and votes consistently with his conscience, whether with or against the ministry." He obviously felt that political party or "faction" control would interfere with the kind of decision the elected official should make — hence the notion of voting with one's conscience. When discussing his ideals as a journalist, Mackenzie said he intended to report on elected representatives and "make known the sentiments of your loyal, honest and independent breasts."

In today's world, Vaclav Havel, the leader of the Velvet Revolution in the 1980s and then president of the Czech Republic, expresses similar views, noting that "loyalty to the party leadership or the party apparatus can count for more than the will of the electorate and the abilities of the politician." He writes, "Gradually the electors may come to be governed by people they did not specifically elect in the first place."

This idea of an elected person deciding to strike out on his or her own and vote according to what seems "right" and "appropriate" is at such a distance from the current practice of government in Canada that many probably find it laughable. The dominance of the political party in decision-making has become so established that alternatives have been squeezed right out.

Yet political parties are not widely loved by the public. The Reform Party in western Canada advocated systems of local recall to temper party influence, but even it was not willing to take the further step advocated by one of the first reformers in Canada: to support real power exercised by an elected individual voting with his or her conscience. This approach would redefine the nature of elected government.

Elections must be free and fair, including a secret ballot.

Many people consider elections the centrepiece of democratic government. They rate elections as much more significant than knowledge of government decisions, access to the documents on which decisions are made, or public input into decisions. In all likelihood they would consider issues of representation and accountability a by-product of the election process. Yet even with the best of election processes, many of these assumptions are contentious or questionable. And many elections are not good processes but badly flawed ones that inspire little confidence.

At least three issues bedevil the election process: who is entitled to vote and which names are actually on the voters list; the time and attention available during the election period for disseminating information and for public discussion and debate; and the resources available to different candidates to communicate with and influence voters. Mackenzie and his colleagues faced all three in the general election in 1836, which Head so deeply interfered with — ensuring that most reformers were not returned — that he provoked the rebellion. These issues have often reared their heads in intervening years, showing how little progress has been made to resolve them in the public interest since Mackenzie began to voice his complaints in the 1820s and '30s.

Mackenzie's complaints about ridings of widely different size, giving some voters more weight than others, have already been cited. These disparities continue. The average population per electoral district in Canada in 1999 was 90,678, but the average population in an electoral district located in the Greater Toronto Area was 101,818, with at least one Toronto riding containing more than 110,000 people — compared with the riding of Cardigan, Prince Edward Island, at 30,058 residents. One vote in Toronto has considerably less weight than one vote anywhere else in the country.

Although all adults who hold citizenship and are resident in the voting district, regardless of gender or property qualification, are eligible to vote, they may not be on the voters list. In 1996 the federal government adopted legislation mandating a permanent voters list to save the costs of doing a door-to-door enumeration of all voters, but in the November 2000 federal election, no fewer than one million people had to take steps to add their names to the voters list when they found they had not been included. One can only assume that several hundred thousand others should have been on the list but weren't.

In the June 1999 provincial election in Ontario, where the same permanent voters list was relied on, the error rate for a multi-unit residential building in downtown Toronto was about 50 per cent: half the names on the list were those of people no longer resident (some had moved away four or five years previously), and half the residents in the building who should have been on the list weren't. Since about 50,000 voters lived in the 47,000 units in multi-unit residential buildings in one riding, this meant that about 25,000 names had been left off the list and 25,000 people not entitled to vote were on the list, amounting to an error rate of almost 40 per cent of those who voted. To ensure that few would complain about the inaccuracy of the voters list, the provincial government had passed legislation effectively silencing those most interested in challenging an inaccurate voters list. It stated, "The permanent register shall be updated with respect to all of Ontario at a registered [political] party's request. However, in that case the costs of updating, as determined by the Chief Election Officer, shall be paid by the party." Updating a voters list would involve door-to-door enumeration at a cost of several million of dollars, a cost that is clearly prohibitive for any political party.

A second issue in ensuring free and fair elections is allowing sufficient time for information, discussion, and debate. Time — a great deal of time — is needed for these processes to occur properly. In Mackenzie's day, there were scarcely a few weeks between the calling of an election and election day. The common practice was for candidates to hold public election meetings at which they would state their views and voters would engage in discussion. Ridings were small enough that a candidate could expect to talk to every voter personally. For example, when Mackenzie ran for the first city council in the general election in March 1834, he received 148 votes, the highest number of any candidate for alderman across the city. Most other candidates for alderman or councillor were elected with fewer than 100 votes.

Today ridings are far larger and the likelihood of a candidate meeting any more than a few thousand voters is remote. There are significant challenges to effective communication, given the great number of commercial advertisers (and other candidates) trying to get the attention of

the same individuals on radio and television and in newspapers. Elections are usually held within twenty-eight
days of being called, and since the calling is at the discretion of the government leader (the precise week and day
is often a surprise), the challenge for a candidate is enormous: rent an election office, arrange for telephones to
be installed, get signs printed, get election pamphlets
printed, and pull together an election organization. By the
time a candidate's team is ready to roll, there is less than
three weeks left in the campaign, a period in which it is
exceedingly difficult to arrange events ensuring widespread debate and a reasonable exchange of information.
The more likely tactic is advertising, where the hope is to
overwhelm the voter rather than attempting to engage and
persuade.

Many candidates have no interest in debate and don't
bother to attend public election meetings. Even party
leaders limit themselves to one or perhaps two heavily
scripted televised debates with their opponents, events
that do nothing to inform candidates of public issues or
public opinions. It is entirely possible that a candidate can
be elected to office without ever having had to defend his
or her position on any matter of substance.

The third election issue is financing. This is not a new
issue, although since Mackenzie's time it has changed
considerably. In his day elections were influenced by candidates and their supporters providing voters with free
alcohol and with small payments in return for votes. In
1836, when Mackenzie and other Reformers failed to be

re-elected, it was widely said that the Family Compact, led by the lieutenant-governor himself, intervened directly in the election through payments, alcohol, and instigated violence, to successfully turn the outcome against the Reformers. With the institution of the secret ballot, buying votes in these ways became much more difficult, since the secrecy of the ballot meant that a candidate could never be sure that the voter's promise was actually kept. Such practices as providing payment for promise of a vote are now codified as criminal activities.

The focus has shifted from actions which would influence individual voters to those which will influence the candidate. Only the winner will hold a seat in the Assembly, so someone looking for influence will provide funds to help ensure the election of a candidate who they expect will work in their interests. Substantial sums are required to conduct elections as they are currently practised, particularly to pay for advertisements and for the advice needed to negotiate the media on a daily basis. Money has an enormous influence on the outcome of elections, which is why many candidates go to great lengths to secure enormous financial resources and why many donors are more than willing to provide funds in the hope of future influence.

In response, most political jurisdictions set rules about political financing, particularly fixing upper limits on donations; controlling the amounts of money that can be spent and the way that it is spent; and making public who gives how much. It is often assumed that if these rules about money apply equally to all political parties, then all parties will have an equal chance, and the quality of democracy will survive intact. It is also assumed that money is needed for election campaigns — apparently a necessary evil — so donors should be encouraged to provide it by subsidization or tax write-offs. This means that the public actually pays for the cost of a good chunk of most election campaigns.

Ontario is generally representative of how things work in most Canadian provinces (except Quebec and Manitoba). In Ontario in 2002, the amount which can be contributed by an individual or a corporation in an election year is $15,000 to each political party; $2,000 to a constituency association of a party, to a maximum of $10,000 to all associations; and $2,000 to a candidate for a political party, to a maximum of $10,000 to all party candidates. These rules permit an individual to give up to $35,000 in an election year to the cause of a particular party. An individual who also happens to control two corporations can make these donations as an individual and as two different corporations, so that the amount contributed to the cause of a particular party by this individual could exceed $100,000, much of which is rebated through public funds. Those controlling more corporations, or arranging for similar donations by spouses, other family members, and employees, can have an even larger financial impact. (Independent candidates are treated as inferior beings when it comes to raising funds and suffer severe limitations in the donations they may receive.)

All donations attract very significant public subsidies, up to 75 per cent of the donation; unused tax credits can be carried forward to future years, and often donations are treated as businesses deductions from Ontario taxes. The result is that almost 90 per cent of the money donated to political parties is actually funded by the public purse, but this expenditure does little to improve public policy or to enhance democratic decision-making. If public funds are as limited as some politicians say, a good place to start the cutbacks might be in this area: stop paying corporations to give money to political parties.

Fundraising is such an important and lucrative activity that parties are constantly doing it through fundraising dinners at a hundred dollars a seat, or perhaps five hundred dollars. Most party leaders spend a third or more of their time fundraising.

The spending of these election finances is controlled only in a formal sense. In Ontario, a political party may spend sixty cents or more per voter, and candidates may spend a further ninety-six cents for every voter in the riding where they are running. But excluded from control are the key elements of a campaign — travel, polling, and research — making a mockery of any serious limit on what can be spent. Further, the upper limits on expenditures have been set so high in Ontario that it is hard to spend all the money raised. Premier Mike Harris raised $6.2 million in the four-week election period in 1999 (that does not include the millions of dollars raised before the election was called), but the party was able to spend only

$5.8 million during those twenty-eight days. Total spending during the whole of 1999 by the Conservatives was $17.9 million.

The Conservatives reported two main areas of expenditure during the campaign. Some $1.3 million was spent on polling, about $40,000 a day, which buys a substantial amount of detailed polling in ridings where the party felt there was a real challenge. The company which undertook much of this work for the Conservatives, Responsive Marketing Group, is understood not to do independent polling by surveying several hundred people in a more or less random way, asking questions, and tabulating results; instead it does telemarketing — that is, making the pitch for a product or a party on the telephone. Elections Ontario reviewed a complaint filed on this matter and responded five months later, stating that it was satisfied the law was not broken, but it would provide no further details.

The second main area of expenditure for the Conservatives was advertising: $3.5 million, almost all of it television advertising, or $170,000 for each of the twenty-one days when television advertising was permitted. This was in addition to the $100 million in public funds spent by the government to tell the public how well it was doing in the previous three years. There is no question but that money spent by a political party has as much influence as money spent on behalf of products during a sales campaign.

The alternative to the Ontario model can be found in

Manitoba and Quebec. In both provinces, donations are limited to three thousand dollars per voter per year, and donations from corporations or non-voters are not permitted. In these jurisdictions political leaders must be serious about engaging members of the public, since it will be impossible to win an election through the limited advertising that the strict donation regime can fund.

If one assumed, as Mackenzie did, that voting was for the purpose of allowing voters to make educated choices, it would be difficult to argue that current practices enhance the voting process. In fact, they might well compromise the election process to such an extent that radical changes may be needed once more to re-establish democratic and responsible government. Clearly, elections alone are not the defining factor of a democracy.

It's difficult to be dispassionate about the current political situation when the distance is so great between it and the one that Mackenzie struggled so hard to bring into being. Measured against the current situation, Mackenzie stands as a beacon of democratic thinking and practice for outlining proposals for action that lie at the root of that political activity.

11 · L'Envoi

I'M BACK IN the cemetery, beside your gravestone, Mackenzie. It's an early February day, cold air, snow that's a few weeks old, hard and crisp, losing its whiteness. There's blue in the sky between the puffy clouds, but the cutting wind holds no hint of spring.

I'm gloomy. My city — your city — has suffered many calamities of late, including the outrageous fortune of forced amalgamation and its financial problems. I'm deeply worried that the energy that you, I, and many, many other people put into this city for the past two hundred years now counts for naught. I can't think of the leaders of the government at Queen's Park as anything other than vandals, and I feel deeply frustrated, and angry.

But let me admit it outright. I'm astounded at how your spirit has invigorated me during the many months that I have been working with your thoughts and your writing to complete this book, struggling to understand the conclusions that others have come to about you in light of what I think I have learned. You've been a powerful inspiration. You have lifted my spirits and helped to clarify my thoughts about the kind of government I want to strive for.

I don't know everything about you I'd like to know. You've kept some secrets. But I understand that's how it is when trying to write about another person. There might be patterns, but never simplicity. There are always loose pieces, surprises, empty sections where conjecture jumps in. What comes across most strongly is your passion, your belief in ordinary people at a time when many others only laughed at that value. And I stand amazed at your alertness to your surroundings and the detailed descriptions you made. They reveal your time and place.

I've learned more than I expected, particularly about the way a responsive and responsible government should function. Most critical are actions which indicate how much individuals in the society are valued. If they are valued, given information, provided the opportunity to digest it through wide-ranging discussion, and then encouraged feed back their opinions to those charged with governing, the result is good and democratic government. All the ideology in the world, all the fine democratic principles mean nothing if these mechanisms are not in place, and too often in the world I live in, they aren't. Governments which don't widely share information, which prevent members of the public from making their views known, which refuse to engage in open debate and discussion — they take their shape from the Family Compact structures you so strongly attacked. I learned that structures allowing the public into the debate are the most critical in the creation of responsive, responsible, democratic, government. Yes, elections are important, but they are not the key element, and as is clear from your time and ours, they can be easily sabotaged by strong forces.

I have rummaged in the writings of many political scientists to discover who shared this vision of how good government works and have found only a few. Ernest Barker, writing in Britain in the early twentieth century, captured better than anyone the flavour of the kind of government you stood for:

> We have to discover a system of government which squares with, and is based upon, the free and full development of human personality — not in some, or even in many, but in all. From this point of view it is not the people, as a people, that matters. It is not the majority, as a majority, that matters. It is each human being, as such.
>
> The form of government we have to find is one which elicits and enlists — or at any rate is calculated to elicit and enlist, so far as is humanly possible — the thought, the will, and the general capacity of every

member. It must be a government depending on mutual
interchange of ideas, on mutual criticism of the ideas
interchanged, and on the common and agreed choice
of the idea which emerges triumphant from the ordeal
of interchange and criticism. A government depending
on such a process can enlist in itself and its own operation the self of every member. It will be self-government: it will be square with, and be based upon, the
development of personality and individuality in every
self. It will be government by the people not as a mass,
or as a majority, but as a society of living selves. In that
sense it will be a democracy. But it will be a democracy
which does not rest on number or mass or quantity. It
will be a democracy which rests on the spiritual quality
of the process which it disengages, and on the value of
the process for every participant.

That process is, in a word, discussion — discussion
of competing ideas, leading to a compromise in which
all the ideas are reconciled and which can be accepted
by all because it bears the imprint of all.

Barker neatly sums up your political style and practice
from the Dundee Rational Institution onwards, but what's
needed to shore up this philosophy is your set of actions,
which made these thoughts so real. You believed ordinary
people are important, their ideas do matter, and that
there's no reason for believing that those who hold public
office are any more intelligent than anyone else, even
though they have the ability to make the final decision.

Dressed in the language of millennium discourse, your ethos would admirably fit that of the philosopher Ronald Beiner, who writes (attributing the idea to Hannah Arendt), "Our prime need as human beings is to be drawn out of ourselves, and to be inserted in a public world of shared experience, shared vocabulary, shared spectacles; for it is mutual involvement in the enacted stories that unfold in our public world that confers meaning upon an existence that might otherwise reduce to senseless drudgery or banality." You recognized that these beliefs are reflected in practice only if government behaviour is structured in a reasonable way. Your thinking needs wide broadcast today, when political leaders are full of democratic bluster and empty of the practice.

What also became clear to me is that the devices in vogue today for government reform are insubstantial compared with your vision of good government. I'm thinking of ideas such as proportional representation and referendums. Proportional representation has been proposed to replace the current voting system, which gives victory to the candidate (usually belonging to a political party) who receives the most votes, even if not a majority of votes in the riding, and gives the voters who opted for another candidate, even if they were a majority of voters, nothing. Proportional representation is determined to find a way around this problem by reserving some seats in the parliament or legislature for representatives of political parties which receive a smaller percentage of vote than the winning party. The hope is that proportional representation will add useful diversity to the political landscape, and indeed it may accomplish that but it does little to give members of the public the opportunity to directly address issues as they arise. It does nothing to ensure that those elected feel they have an obligation to listen to and act upon expressed opinions. You would have had great trouble supporting proportional representation.

You would also have had a low opinion of polls and referendums, since you believed that public issues were best resolved by an informed public engaging in substantial public debate. It was from that debate that educated people could form their own opinions. The best strategies and proposals emerged from social interaction, and you seemed to see no shortcut past that process.

These two devices are trumpeted as necessary reforms today because of the control exerted by political parties and their leaders on the structures of public governance. On this subject you were crystal clear: political factions and parties were an anathema. Your strong opinions are reflected now by Vaclav Havel. Havel spent time in a Czechoslovakian jail until the rulers were overthrown in the late 1980s; then, quite quickly, he became president of the country. You'd like his words:

> It would seem to make more sense if ... people rather than political parties were elected (that is, if people could be elected without party affiliation).... Parties should not take direct part in elections, nor should they be allowed to give anyone, a priori, the crutches of

power. In other words, they should not participate directly in power, since when they do they inevitably become bureaucratic, corrupt, and undemocratic.

Would it be possible to create a political party on the basis of your principles for action, in lieu of the more traditional list of economic, social, and health policies? Could one have a party whose members promised allegiance to the following ideas?

- I commit myself to ensure that full information on public issues is publicly available in a timely fashion.

- I will ensure that there is adequate time and opportunity for public discussion and debate of important issues before decisions are finalized by elected officials, and that I will play an active part in facilitating that debate.

- I will ensure that there are good opportunities for members of the public to make their views known at times and places convenient to them, and specifically that committees of the legislature will be used for such hearings, and I commit myself to listen closely and attentively to public debate and public input.

- I commit myself to vote and act in ways which, according to my conscience, best embody and express the public good.

- I will work to ensure that elections are free and fair expressions of an informed public.

One can imagine this kind of platform holding some attraction for a political party — a party of individuals who share a loyalty to ordinary people and the power of debate, rather than to a party leader. Would you lead such a party?

Perhaps you believe all parties would quickly become Family Compacts. They certainly come to embody ideologies, since any group of people is most easily controlled by a few overarching ideas to which individuals are subservient. Our friend Barker said, "As soon as any political party begins to believe that it is the sole possessor of an exclusive truth, democracy is already dying or dead; and it is only a formal registration of its death if such a party proceeds to act in the logic of its belief, and to suppress other parties on the ground that they believe in falsehood, and there is no truth in them. There cannot be any discussion, or any system of government by discussion, except upon the assumption that truth dwells in more than one habitation, and that its elements have to be collected, and not only collected but reconciled, before it can be enthroned." I can't believe you'd disagree.

And there's another idea I see emerging from your remarks, particularly what you wrote from jail in Rochester in December 1840: "My creed has been social democracy — or equality of each man before society — and political democracy, or the equality of each man before the law." The two equalities go together: democratic decision-making fails when those in power conclude that the concerns of some people (usually those at the bottom end of the economy) are undeserving of reasonable consideration.

Valuing individuals in the decision-making process means they must be valued in the economy. When the poor are demonized, when programs serving them are pulled out without replacement, when they are set upon by a mounting array of rules and regulations and given no grounds for recourse — then the democratic approach is in danger. Democracy rests on valuing each member of society. It is no accident that the leaders who take an ideological approach ("We know the answers") first attack the poor, then remove the mechanisms for democratic discussion. Your belief in social justice and democracy was all of one piece, as it must be.

I am moved by a poem found among your papers. It was written by David Willson, leader of the Children of Peace, who built the extraordinary temple at Sharon, an hour's drive north of Toronto. I have visited the Sharon Temple on many occasions and only recently discovered your notes about visiting the site as its four wooden walls were being raised in the late summer of 1828. "One thing is evident," you wrote after looking at what they had done, "they afford ample proofs, both in their village and in that chapel, that comparatively great achievements may be accomplished by a few when united in their efforts and preserving in their habits and systems."

The poem was dated by Willson at Sharon on May 22, 1842, when you were in sad exile in New York. But you noted the words:

We are all equal in our birth
We're so by God's decree
'Tis but presumtion on the earth
To tread on equity

The last verse reads:

A title's but an empty name
We lose it with our breath:
To earth we all return again —
We're equal in our death

Your sense of equality didn't seek the lowest common denominator, but strove for the highest common factor. It's how you saw good government working, Mackenzie.

Barker concluded his meditation on democracy by postulating three axioms which I'm sure you'd agree to,

There are thus three axioms which have to be accepted and obeyed if government by discussion is to work successfully — the axiom of Agreement to Differ: the axiom of the Rule of the Majority: the axiom of Compromise. The central axiom is that of majority-rule; and it is natural to concentrate attention upon that axiom. But it is only one of three; and it is lame and halt without the other two....

If Majority-rule is combined with agreement to differ and compromise, there will be no tyranny of the majority. The majority will not only agree to differ from the minority — tolerating, and even encouraging, the existence of opposition because opposition is necessary to the health of its own existence. It will also make concessions to the views of the minority....

The intransigence which vindicates all action for the majority, and assigns nothing but suffering to minorities, is fatal to the essence of democracy, because it is fatal to discussion. It is an intransigence based upon the conviction that truth is a monopoly, and that a single side alone possesses "the truth, the whole truth, and nothing but the truth." When that conviction is entertained, there is no point in discussion and no reason for democracy....

You provoke many deep thoughts, Mackenzie, about the nature of good government and the human condition. I find it's hard to discover a better master than you. Yes, your life was messy, sometimes you lost your way, your family suffered for your dedication, but so often you were clear and challenging. We are so much in debt to you. You cleared the path, even if we have strayed into ground that is barren for good government.

Here, in the cemetery, the cold wind picks up, the winter afternoon is waning. So many political leaders seem so tiny in their puffery compared with you in your threadbare coat, your red wig, your angry eye. Your wisdom continues down through the years. Now, I take my leave. Others will hear your strong voice. Mackenzie, come again. There is much to be done.

Afterword: Searching for Mackenzie in Scotland

TRYING TO PIN DOWN information about Mackenzie in Scotland proved to be very difficult. My interest was specifically to look at material which would bear on the hypothesis that Mackenzie learned about publishing and political activity in Scotland and elsewhere in the United Kingdom.

In September 2000 I was giving a speech in Edinburgh to those involved with the city's World Heritage Trust. At a cocktail party, I introduced myself to Charles McKean, the eminent architectural historian of Scotland's cities. I told him of my interest in Mackenzie and of my intention to visit Dundee, and asked who I might speak to. He immedi-

ately suggested one Henny King, a Canadian living in
Dundee who knew much about the man. I had an address
for her, but no phone number. On a rainy day, the last day
before having to return to Canada, we set out for Dundee,
found the country house in which her flat was located and
rang the buzzer. She considered my request to talk with
her and kindly invited us in for tea. She hailed originally
from Montreal, but had a special interest in Mackenzie,
and was very helpful. Within 15 minutes she had put us in
touch with the Dundee city archivist and other city officials — they were kind enough to remount, in time for my
return visit several months later, the historical marker to
Mackenzie that had been taken down for the construction of
the Overgate shopping mall a decade earlier.

Later that afternoon, at the suggestion of the city
archivist, I visited the university archives where a sign
reading 'Closed for stock-taking' was posted. I pushed
through the door and was met by a young man who told
me the archives were closed. I quickly conveyed my interest in William Lyon Mackenzie and he said "That name
rings a bell. Last night I couldn't sleep, and I picked up a
19th century history of Dundee and I'm sure I came
across his name, but the book is at home by my bed. Give
me your e-mail address and I'll send you the reference."
As it turned out, the Mackenzie reference involved the
Dundee Rational Institute, and as hopefully has been
clear, it was promising. It was on the basis of such mar-
vellous happenstance that the research unfolded, and any
return trip in early 2001 was arranged.

I started by looking at Mackenzie's departure from Scotland. He said that he left in April 1820 from Glasgow, sailing on the *Psyche*. I was interested in trying to find the precise date in April, since it would allow me to fit the departure into the intense political activity occurring in the Glasgow area around that time.

The Archive Room of the Mitchell Library in Glasgow holds the registry kept by the Glasgow port authority, which records boats coming and going from the harbour. Listed are the dates of arrival and departure, the name of the boat, the captain, and the goods carried. The registry shows no listing for a *Psyche* during March, April, or May, 1820, nor for the person Mackenzie named as its captain, Thomas Erskine.

Newspapers for the same period often carried advertisements of departure dates in order to attract bookings. The two Glasgow newspapers of the day were the *Glasgow Herald* and the *Glasgow Courier*. The local history room of the Mitchell Library has both papers on microfiche. Neither paper has an advertisement for the *Psyche* during this period.

The other major harbour in the Glasgow area in 1820 was Greenock, about twenty miles down the Clyde River. Attempts to locate a port registry for Greenock were unsuccessful; according to Peter Summerville of the Greenock Ocean Terminal — the current port authority — no such registry exists. The newspaper of the period was the *Greenock Advertiser and Clyde Commercial Herald*, published twice a week. It lists the ships "Arrived" and

"Sailed," and the captains' names. Microfiche for this newspaper is available at the James Watt Library in Greenock (where there is a very large statue of James Watt), but no *Psyche* is mentioned during March, April, or May 1820.

Some information regarding boats, including port registries, is in the control of the National Archives of Scotland. A later visit to the West Register in Charlotte Square, Edinburgh, where shipping registries are kept, did not turn up a registry for Greenock. The West Register noted that the Glasgow registry had been returned to the Mitchell Library, as I had already learned. No listing for a captain named Thomas Erskine was found in biographical reference books in the Mitchell Library.

Several archivists I talked to said that there seem to be many examples of boats known to have been in a certain harbour but not included in registries. It is entirely possible that Mackenzie was correct in saying that he left aboard the *Psyche* in April 1820, even though this is not recorded anywhere.

Registry records for the year 1820 in Quebec, which is where Mackenzie landed, have not been found. The Quebec Port Authority does not have such records and indicates that if they are anywhere, they would be in the National Archives of Canada. They do not appear to be in said archives in Ottawa.

The Glasgow and Greenock newspapers were full of news of the political turmoil in this part of Scotland during March and April 1820, and they report many instances of

Radicals operating in the area. Anyone in the vicinity
would have been fully aware of what was going on, since
it was common knowledge both to those reading newspapers and to those walking along the road. However,
newspapers of the day rarely mentioned the names of
those involved: there was no mention of either Mackenzie
or the friend with whom he left for Canada, John Lesslie.

It is a moot question whether some English archive
contains notes about those involved in the uprising. Two
historians of the period (Professor Ted Cowan, Chair of
the Department of Scottish History, Glasgow University;
and Professor Chris Whatley, Chair of the History
Department, Dundee University) both thought that Lord
Sidmouth and other English authorities took advantage of
the political fervour and made extensive use of *agents
provocateurs* to heighten sentiments in a way that would
allow them to rush in and make arrests to put down real
reform. If the English authorities played such a powerful
role in provoking the uprising, they would have had good
reason to avoid writing down any instructions or commu-
nications in order to protect the identity of their spies.
This means that the chance of finding detailed information on those involved in planning the uprising is probably
very limited. Trying to pin down Mackenzie in this way
would most likely be a fruitless task.

One local historian (John Brims, the archivist in charge
of the Stirling Archives) suggested that the Scottish Radical
movement of this period was very broad and included a
vast range of temperaments and strategies, and that only

a small element was involved in strategies that included violence. Scottish radicals who shared a belief in the integrity and worth of the individual but not a proclivity to violence might have looked with interest on the insurrection while still keeping their distance. It would be unlikely that such Radicals would become part of the documentation of the English authorities, which presents a further difficulty in tracing names.

I looked for Mackenzie's involvement in Dundee. The Local Studies Room of the Dundee Central Library has a copy of "The Laws and Regulations of the Dundee Rational Institution," printed in 1813 by Rintoul (see Chapter 2). It also has microfiche copies of the *Dundee Advertiser* for the period as well as the newspaper's centenary booklet issued in 1901.

Selected issues of the *Advertiser* were reviewed to determine whether Mackenzie might for some reason be mentioned. One local opportunity was in early 1817. George Kinloch chaired a meeting on January 24, 1817, at the Morrens Hotel in Dundee in honour of the liberal Charles James Fox. The meeting resulted in a petition submitted a few weeks later to city council, asking it to sponsor a meeting on parliamentary reform. The meeting was reported in the *Advertiser* on January 31, but the only persons mentioned besides Kinloch were David Jobson, Robert Bell, J.G. Rossell, and Robert Modie.

The petition attracted 110 signatories, and I wondered whether Mackenzie would be among them. Iain Flett, the archivist at the Dundee City Archives, was quickly able to produce the city council minute book, and the minutes note that the petition was submitted to council on February 8, 1817. The petition was reported in the *Advertiser* on February 14, without mention of the signatories. Unfortunately, the petition itself has been lost, probably having been burned in a fire that occurred in 1931 when the former City Hall was demolished.

One father of reform, Major John Cartwright, came to Dundee for a meeting in August 1815. The *Advertiser* reported the visit in the September 1, 1815 issue, but no names are mentioned of those with whom Cartwright met. (On September 8, 1815, the *Advertiser* reported that Cartwright, Frances Burdet, and several others held a meeting in Glasgow on parliamentary reform and that "the hall was so crowded at an early hour that an immense number who came forward found it impossible to gain admittance.")

Mackenzie's relationship with the *Advertiser* remains unclear. He said he was often in the reading room of the newspaper and he had a friendly relationship with the editor, Robert Rintoul. The *Advertiser* has been in continuous publication since Mackenzie's day, now operating under the name of the *Dundee Courier*. During my visit to Dundee in January 2001, the newspaper was celebrating its two-hundredth birthday. The journalist considered to be the newspaper's historian, Norman Watson, said that there were no records from the 1820s about who was employed by or writing for the newspaper.

I attempted to explore the business relationship that

Mackenzie had with Edward Lesslie, since Lesslie's son said Mackenzie was his father's employee, although this was never confirmed by Mackenzie. Mackenzie ran a shop in Alyth, outside Dundee, for several years until its bankruptcy in 1815 or 1816. I wondered if perhaps Edward Lesslie had loaned Mackenzie money for this shop, or for the shop that Mackenzie then established in Dundee, since Lesslie had apparently provided the capital for his sons to establish the shops in Upper Canada. Iain Flett of the Dundee City Archives noted that loans were required at that time to be registered, and he produced the loan registries for the period 1810 to 1817. There was no record of any loan from Edward Lesslie or of any loan to Mackenzie. It may not be fair to conclude that no loan was made; perhaps it was made but not registered.

Professor Chris Whatley suggested that there may have been a record of Mackenzie being involved in the riot in December 1816 in Dundee. There is evidence that planning preceded the event, the proximate cause of which was an increase in the price of cornmeal. Often the government investigated these instances of social unrest, and I took up his suggestion of visiting the National Archives in Edinburgh to look into this.

In the West Register in Charlotte Square, Edinburgh, I discovered the records of the lord advocate's department in the early nineteenth century. Three "precognitions" were undertaken into this event — that is, evidence statements from witnesses, taken under oath, catalogued as AD 14, 16/52, 56, and 58. There are about three-hundred foolscap pages in all, summarizing the evidence of forty or fifty witnesses. There is no mention of Mackenzie.

My wife, Elizabeth Rykert, was a great help and inspiration in undertaking this research in Scotland, as well as being a terrific travel companion. It was the first time we had done serious archival work, and we both found it entrancing. We held in our hands documents that were almost two hundred years old and reflected on the lives of those writing, or asking questions, or answering.

For lack of serious leads in London, no work was done there on the eighteen months Mackenzie allegedly spent in the city. Internet contact with the Kennet and Avon canal company was unsuccessful; it is unclear whether the company would have any records which clarified how Mackenzie managed to find work with them. For his 1987 article, F.K. Donnelly looked for Mackenzie records among the Lonsdale papers, without success.

Endnotes

Chapter 1

PAGE 9. The Kilbourn quote is from page 133 of *The Firebrand;*
the Salutin quote is from page 95.
Armstrong's names and phrases about Mackenzie are spread
through Part II of *City in the Making.*

PAGE 10. Lee's poem, *W.L.M./1838,* is in Kilbourn's *The Toronto Book,*
p. 31.

PAGE 11. The elusiveness of fairly defining 'democracy' can be seen
leafing through C.B. MacPherson's famous *The Real World of
Democracy.*

PAGE 12. Havel's quote is from *Disturbing the Peace,* p. 72.

Chapter 2

PAGE 14. Those relying on these statements of loyalty include Lindsey (Chapter 2), Donnelly, Kilbourn, and Raible, among others.

PAGES 14–15. Mackenzie's quotes come from Lindsey, pp. 37–38.

PAGE 16. Mackenzie's disclaimers about Spafield are from *Colonial Advocate*, 18 May 1824.

PAGE 17. Dundee's radical ethos is best described in Oglivy's article "The Radical Toun," from which comes the quote on socialism and nationalism.

PAGE 18. Rintoul's connection with Dundee radicals is described by Tennant, p. 70, and p. 81.

PAGE 19. Attempts were made to learn about the management of the paper in the early 1800s, including an interview on January 17, 2001 with Norman Watson of the *Dundee Courier* (the successor to the *Advertiser*). Watson was the paper's resident historian, responsible for information relating to the paper's 200th anniversary which occurred a week after this interview. No records from the early 19th century are extant.

The quote from the Institution's booklet is from p.14. The booklet is available in the Local History Room of the Dundee Central Library.

PAGE 20. Rintoul's friends are described on pp. 14–16 of the *Dundee Advertiser, 1801–1901, A centenary memoir*.

Donnelly includes the quote comparing the two newspapers, p. 69, and the visit of Mackenzie to Rintoul, p. 68.

PAGE 21. Donnelly charts the relationship between Mackenzie and the Lesslie family, p. 67. The reference to Mackenzie as a Lesslie employee is from Newcome, p. 20. The diary entry is Dec.6, 1831, and the diary is found in the Dundas Historical Society Museum.

PAGE 22. Peterloo is described by E.P. Thompson, p. 754.

The quote about rebellion is from Ellis, p. 131. Kinloch's biography is Tennant's, *The Radical Laird*.

PAGE 23. For the Cato Street Conspiracy, see Thompson, p. 775.

The Glasgow uprising is described by Whatley, *Scottish Society,* pp. 318–19; and by Ellis. The proclamation is from Ellis, pp. 22–23.

PAGE 24. Copies of the *Glasgow Herald* are lodged in the Glasgow Central Library.

PAGE 25. Further explanation of the tracing of boat traffic can be found in the Afterword.

PAGE 26. The claim that Mackenzie fled is from Ellis, p. 293, but Donnelly notes (p. 70) that it is unsubstantiated.

The difficulty in learning the real story about the uprising is noted by Whatley in *Scottish Society,* pp. 318–19.

Donnelly puts Mackenzie in Dundee in November 1819, p. 68.

Mackenzie's fondness for play is noted by Lindsey, p. 33.

PAGE 27. Lindsey cites the relationship with Lord Lowther, p. 42.

Lowther is best described in *British Biographical Archive.*

Donnelly found no record of Lowther employing Mackenzie, footnote 13, p. 71. Donnelly describes the assignation with the Duc, p. 68.

PAGE 29. Mackenzie's praise of Kinlock is found in *Colonial Advocate,* 2 June 1833. The *Advocate*'s report is found in the West Register, National Archives, Edinburgh.

PAGE 30. Mackenzie's comment on Cobbett is from *Colonial Advocate,* 15 November 1832.

PAGE 32. Mackenzie's shifting views are derided by Rasporich, p. 5.

The quote about Cobbett and his policies is from Thompson, p. 820.

The quote about Cobbett's influence (cont. pp. 33–34) is from p. 823.

PAGE 34. The quote beginning 'Deficient in theory' is from Thompson, p. 833.

PAGE 35. The Mackenzie material is in the Mackenzie File 850, Ontario Archives, Toronto.

PAGE 36. Mackenzie becoming a U.S. citizen is noted by Luno, p. 15.

Chapter 3

PAGE 38. The quote opening the chapter is from *The Constitution,* 21 December 1836.

PAGE 39. The Montreal period is described in DCB, Vol. 9, p. 497.

PAGE 40. The family situation is described by Raible in *Muddy York Mud*, p. 33.

Newcome argues Mackenzie was a manager in Dundas, p. 20; Raible, in his *Colonial Advocate*, p. 17, that he was a partner. The two also differ about the reasons for leaving Dundas.

PAGE 41. Luno argues for Randall's influence in establishing a newspaper, p. 3.

Raible notes the 'patron is the people' in his *Colonial Advocate*, p. 20. The quote about 'doing the people's business' is from *Colonial Advocate*, 22 September 1831.

The quotes about the *Mercury* are from *Colonial Advocate*, 22 September 1831.

PAGE 42. The names and the quote are in the first issue of *Colonial Advocate*, 18 May 1824. The print run is from Raible's pamphlet, *WL Mackenzie, Printer*.

PAGE 45. The dream of the mild and amiable governor is from *Colonial Advocate*, 9 February 1825. The story about Bidwell is from the issue of 4 November 1824.

PAGE 46. The attack by the *Gazette* is noted by Raible in his *Colonial Advocate*, p. 38.

PAGE 47. The 'free discussion' quote is from *Colonial Advocate*, 10 June 1824.

The Dalton quote about the junto is noted by Patterson.

Bidwell's quote is from Wallace, pp. 3–4.

PAGE 49. The 'profiteering' words come from Salutin, p. 57. The 'vindictive family faction' is from *Colonial Advocate*, 3 November 1831.

PAGES 50–53. The description of the Family Compact appeared in a Supplement to the *Advocate*, 26 September 1833.

PAGE 54. The 'thirty tyrants' quote was in the *Correspondent and Advocate*, 3 December 1835.

PAGE 55. The quote about informing people was published in *The Constitution*, 21 December 1836.

PAGE 56. The satire about the legislators in the hospital was in *Colonial Advocate*, 20 January 1825.

PAGE 57. The story of the paper mills is from Darke, *A Mill Should Be Thereon*, pp. 53–55.

The newspaper circulation figures are from Lindsey, p. 108.

PAGE 58. Raible concludes the Swift satires were sometimes nasty, *Muddy York Mud*, p. 26.

PAGE 59. Raible gives an entertaining context for and account of the break-in in *Muddy York Mud*.

PAGE 60. The reference to Jarvis taking the blame is in Raible, *Muddy York* Mud, p. 236.

Chapter 4

PAGE 63. Regarding Thorpe succeeding Weekes, see Wilton, pp. 24–27. Further material on Thorpe is from DCB, VII, p. 864. On Willcocks, see DCB V, p. 854 and Clark, pp. 213–15.

PAGE 64. Information on Gourlay is from Milani and from DCB, Vol IX, p. 330. For those words in the questionnaire, see Milani, pp. 98–99.

PAGE 65. Regarding the use of township meetings, see Carol Wilton, passim. For Gourlay as a demagogue, see Hume, pp. 9–19.

The quote about the constitution being in danger is from Milani, p. 138.

PAGE 66. Robinson's quote about the effectiveness of the meetings is from Clark, p. 341.

PAGE 67. For those elected after Gourlay, see Clarke p. 348.

Mackenzie describes the legislation and quotes from it in *Colonial Advocate*, 10 January 1833. Robinson's quote about Mackenzie is from Brode, p. 113.

PAGE 68. Wise makes the critical quote about Gourlay in DCB, p. 334.

More critical is John Fraser in *Eminent Canadians*, pp. 48–55.

Kilbourn discusses the younger Baldwin, *The Firebrand*, pp. 47–48.

PAGE 69. Wilton notes the land situation, p. 35. Nichol's role in the alien question is described by Milani, pp. 92–95.

PAGE 70. Two who noted that Mackenzie learned from this petition are
Lindsey, pp. 139–145, and Wallace, pp. 63–65.

PAGE 71. The perfect representative is described in *Colonial Advocate*,
18 May 1824.

PAGE 72. The long quote about the patriot is from *Colonial Advocate*,
4 May 1825.

PAGE 74. The letter to the electors was published in *Colonial Advocate*,
3 January 1828.

PAGE 76. The description of the nomination is from *Colonial Advocate*,
2 February 1828.

PAGE 78–79. Lindsey describes the committee work, pp. 153–54,
as does Kilbourn, *The Firebrand*, p. 53.

PAGE 80. Lindsey sets the rejected bills at this number, p. 71.
Le Sueur remarks on the power of the councils, p. 122.
Lord Durham's statement is from Lindsey, p. 63.

PAGE 82. For Mackenzie's relationship with Jackson, see Gates' article,
'The Decided Policy of William Lyon Mackenzie,' and Hume, p. 15.
For family details, see Luno.

Chapter 5

PAGE 85. The quote about 'enlightened people' is from *Colonial
Advocate*, 9 September 1830, as is the quote on page 86, 'Beware of
secret associations.'

PAGE 86. Wallace discusses the Reformers' limitations,
[JS1] pp. 72–73.

PAGE 87. Kilbourn uses the 'little mannikin' reference on p. 56,
The Firebrand.

PAGE 88. Dent quotes Mackenzie on the use of published proceedings
to educate the public. p. 237.

PAGE 89. The Everlasting Salary Bill is discussed in the DCB entry on
Mackenzie, p. 499.
Mackenzie's quotes about representation come from *Colonial
Advocate*, 3 February 1831.

PAGE 90. Quotes about the immigrant ship are from *Colonial Advocate*, 20 May and 9 June 1831.

PAGE 92. The discouraged historian is Gates, attempting to sum up Aileen Dunham in her article 'The Decided Policy of William Lyon Mackenzie.'

PAGE 93. The MANY and the FEW is from *Colonial Advocate*, 11 August 1831. The petition was published in *Colonial Advocate*, 21 July 1831.

PAGE 94. Mackenzie's statement in the Legislature is in a footnote in Lindsey, pp. 182–84.

PAGES 95–96. Mackenzie's report, and the names he was called, are in a footnote in Lindsey, pp. 185 – 201.

PAGE 97. Voting day on January 2 is described by Lindsey, p. 205. The results of the January 30 election are described by Wallace, p. 81.

PAGE 99. The London scene is from *Colonial Advocate*, 13 September 1832.

PAGE 101. For Ryerson's intervention, see Brown, p. 143, and Craig's *Upper Canada: The Formative Years*, p. 216. Mackenzie's meeting with Cobbett is from *Colonial Advocate*, 15 November 1832.

PAGE 102. Wallace uses the phrase an 'outrageous doctrine' on p. 83.

PAGE 103. Hagerman's reappointment is described by Luno, p. 6, as is the dropping of 'Colonial' from the paper's name. The melee in the Legislature is described by Wallace, p. 87

Chapter 6

PAGE 105. Mackenzie's quote about politics is from *Colonial Advocate*, 27 June 1833, and is quoted in part by Lindsey, pp. 284–86.

PAGE 107. A good description of the restructuring debate is in Romney, *Forging a Consensus*, pp. 19–23.

PAGE 109. Mackenzie's quotes about the legislation and the meeting called to discuss it, are from *Advocate*, 20 March 1834.

PAGE 110. The results of the vote for council are tabulated in Romney, *Consensus*, p. 22. Romney generally is helpful describing Mackenzie's term as mayor.

PAGE 111. The quote about the impact of the results on the Family Compact is from Romney, *Consensus*, p. 34. The financial impacts on restructuring are noted in Romney's article in *Canadian Historical Review*, p. 416.

PAGE 112. The assessment differentials are from Romney, *Consensus*, pp. 23–24.

The difficulty in securing a loan are noted by Armstrong, p. 109.

PAGE 114. Romney deals with the Hume letter in *Consensus*, p. 25.

PAGE 116. The quote about Mackenzie as a good mayor is from Romney in *Canadian Historical Review*, p. 434.

Chapter 7

PAGE 120. The three types of witnesses are described in the *Select Committee Report*, pp. xxx–xxxi.

PAGE 121. The reference to the 1828 report is found on p. ii.

The quote about unlimited patronage is on p. iii, with specifics continuing to p. viii.

PAGE 123. The quote about the need to have a non-partisan judiciary is from p. xxxviii–xxxix. The quotes about the Legislative Council are from p. xxxix–xl.

PAGE 124. The quote about how badly Upper Canada has been governed is from pp. xxxix–xli.

PAGE 125. The quote about the lieutenant governor is from pp. xxxix–xli.

PAGE 126. The quote about about the Assembly is from p. xlviii.

PAGE 127. Luno deals with his appointment to the Welland Canal Board, p. 7.

Kilbourn has a good description of the appointments to the Executive Council, Chapt. 11, *The Firebrand*.

PAGE 128. Wallace sets out the Assembly resolution, p. 105.

PAGE 129. Kilbourn cites the letters about the impact of Head's decisions, pp. 140–41, *The Firebrand.*

PAGE 130. The intimidation is noted by Dent, p. 329, and the gangsterism by Ryerson, p. 117. The influence of Hume's letter is noted by
Dent, p. 333.

PAGE 131. The failure of Mackenzie's challenge to the vote because of
the Clerk's bad advice is noted by Dent, pp. 348–49.

PAGE 132. Mackenzie's quote about the source of his strength is from
The Constitution, 8 February 1837. His travel to New York is noted
by Wallace, p. 115.
Mackenzie's hope for the English Reformers is noted in Hume,
pp. 9–19.

PAGE 133. Mackenzie's quote about the need for meetings comes from
The Constitution, 24 May 1837, as does the long excerpt about the
people of Upper Canada.

PAGE 135. The quote including 'Justice Shall Reign' is from
The Constitution, 26 July 1837.

Chapter 8

PAGE 136. Guillet, in *Lives of the Patriots*, p. 10, claims that Mackenzie
attended 200 meetings, but that is not sourced, and is surely a
significant overstatement. More likely Mackenzie attended a meeting every second or third day during the summer and early fall.

PAGE 137. The long quote about revolutionary change is from
The Constitution, 26 July 1837.

PAGE 139. The resolution at the August meeting is printed in *The
Constitution*, 2 August 1837, and discussed by Craig, pp. 208–212.

PAGE 140. The threat to Mackenzie's life is noted in Guillet, pp. 10–11.
The support of Rolph, Morrison, and Fletcher is documented by
Read and Stagg. Mackenzie's puffing of support is noted by Wallace,
p. 126.

PAGE 142. Kilbourn mentions Hume's example, *The Firebrand*, p. 152.

PAGE 143. Explanation of the role of Gurnett is found in Russell's
Mayors of Toronto, pp. 25–27.

PAGES 143–49. The broadsheet is from Lindsey, vol.II, Appendix F.

PAGE 150. Salutin has a fairly reliable step-by-step recounting of events, p. 126f, but it should be augmented, and in some cases modified, by the detail in Read and Stagg.

PAGE 151. Powell's statement that he was never asked about a gun comes from Read and Stagg, p. 136.

PAGE 157. The quote from Mackenzie about common people putting themselves at risk for him is recounted by Salutin, p. 142.

PAGE 158. Salutin's comments about punishment, pp. 158–163, is not entirely correct. Read and Stagg provide more reliable data. Many of the events leading to individuals being put to death or transported had to do with later cross-border raids, not with rebellious activity within Upper Canada.

Chapter 9

Gates provides a very detailed and reliable book about Mackenzie's life after the rebellion, both in the States and later in Canada, and it has been used extensively in this chapter.

PAGE 160. Head's quotes about democracy come from Head's narrative. This first quote is from p. 40.

PAGE 161. Head's quote about the 'insane theory of conciliating democracy,' is from pp. 20–21.

PAGE 162. Head's quote about how much Upper Canadians hate democracy is from p. 66.

PAGE 163. The quotes about the meaning of democracy come from Butler, pp. 240–41.
Mackenzie's quote about social and political democracy is from *Mackenzie's Gazette*, 23 December 1840.

PAGE 164. Gates recounts the American citizenship episode, p. 41.

PAGE 165. Gates' observation of Mackenzie's behaviour at his trial is from p. 64. The strength of the petition to release Mackenzie is noted by Salutin, p. 168.

PAGE 168. Mackenzie's lament for his daughter is noted by Luno, p.19.

A brief description of the Rebellion Losses Bill is found in the Canadian Encyclopedia, p. 1550.

PAGE 169. Luno recounts the move back to Toronto, p.24.

Careless describes Toronto in 1850 in *Toronto to 1918*.

PAGE 174. Brown's eulogy on Mackenzie was in the *Globe*, August 29, 1861.

Chapter 10

PAGE 179. The quote about the value of information is by Glorianne Stromberg, former Ontario Securities Commissioner, in the *Globe and Mail*, page A12, October 25, 1999.

PAGE 182. The incidence of the use of time allocation was research done by the author.

PAGE 184. Bill 25, the *Fewer Municipal Politicians Act*, was given third reading by the Legislature on December 20, 1999.

PAGES 185–86. The Mackenzie quotes are from *Colonial* Advocate, 4 May 1825; and 28 October 1824.

PAGE 186. Havel's quote comes from *Summer Meditations*, pp. 54–55.

PAGE 188. The *Toronto Star* deals with the issue of riding size in 'Political Clout', October 9, 1999, p. A29.

PAGE 189. The research about the accuracy of the voters' list was done by the author in the riding of Toronto Centre-Rosedale. Section 17.1(1)(3)3 of the Elections Act contains the amazing provision that in Ontario a political party must pay for an accurate voters' list. This section was enacted in 1998.

Mackenzie's vote is recounted by Romney in *Consensus*, p. 22.

PAGE 194. Spending by Mike Harris and the Progressive Conservative Party of Ontario is reported in John Ibbitson's column, *Globe and Mail*, December 9, 1999, page A4. Total spending was reported by *Toronto Star*, June 3, 2000, p. A3.

The data about spending on 'polling' was noted in *NOW Magazine*, Toronto, January 20–26, 2000, p. 24. The complaint about the matter to Elections Ontario was made by the author.

Chapter 11

PAGES 198–199. The quote about democracy as discussion is from Sir Ernest Barker, *Reflections on Government*, pp. 36–37.

PAGE 200. Beiner's quote is from pp. 184–85.

PAGE 201. One helpful book on proportional representation is *Citizenship and Democracy, A Case for Proportional Representation*, by Nick Loenen. Ideas on that and other ways to put 'democracy' in place are outlined in Judy Rebbicks' book *Imagine Democracy*. For the devastation referendums cause to public governance, see Peter Schrag's book on experience in California, *Paradise Lost*.

PAGE 201–02. Havel's quote is from *Disturbing the Place*, pp. 16–17.

PAGE 203. Barker's quote is from pp. 70–71.

Mackenzie's quote about democracy is from *Gazette*, 23 December 1840.

PAGE 204. Mackenzie wrote about the construction of the Sharon Temple in *Colonial Advocate*, 18 and 25 September 1828.

PAGE 205. Barker's three axioms are from pp. 69–71.

Bibliography

Armstrong, Frederick H., *A City in the Making: Progress, People and Perils in Victorian Toronto*. Dundurn Press, 1988.

Barker, Sir Ernest, *Reflections on Government*. London: Oxford University Press, 1942.

Beiner, Ronald, *Philosophy in a Time of Lost Spirit*. Toronto: University of Toronto Press, 1997.

Brode, Patrick, *Sir John Beverley Robinson: Bone and Sinew of the Compact*. Toronto: published for Osgoode Society by University of Toronto Press, 1984.

Brown, George W., "The Durham Report and the Upper Canadian Scene," *Canadian Historical Review*, June 1939, pp. 136–160.

Bryce, James, *Modern Democracies*. New York: Macmillan, 1921.

Bumsted, J.M., editor, *Canadian History Before Confederation: Essays and Interpretations.* Georgetown, Ont: Irwin-Dorsey, 1972.

Butler, J. R. M., *Passing of the Great Reform Bill.* London: Longmans, Green, 1914.

Careless, J.M.S, *Toronto to 1918: An Illustrated History.* Toronto: James Lorimer & Company, 1984.

——, editor, *The Pre-Confederation Premiers: Ontario Government Leaders 1841–1867.* Toronto: University of Toronto Press, 1980.

Clarke, S.D., *Movements of Political Protest in Canada, 1640–1840.* Toronto: University of Toronto Press, 1939.

Clew, Kenneth R., *The Kennet and Avon Canal.* Newton Abbott: David & Charles, 1973.

Colombo, John Robert, *The Mackenzie Poems: William Lyon Mackenzie and John Robert Colombo.* Toronto: Swan Publishing Company, 1966.

Colonial Advocate: various articles. Ontario Archives.

Craig, Gerald M., "The American Impact on the Upper Canadian Reform Movement Before 1837," *Canadian Historical Review,* XXXIX (1948), pp. 333–352.

——, editor, *Discontent in Upper Canada.* Vancouver: Copp Clark Publishing, 1974.

——, editor, *Lord Durham's Report: An Abridgment.* Toronto: McClelland and Stewart, 1963.

——, *Upper Canada, The Formative Years, 1784–1841.* Toronto: McClelland and Stewart, 1966.

Darke, Eleanor, *A Mill Should Be Thereon.* Toronto: Natural History/Natural Heritage, for East York Historical Society, 1995.

——, and Karadi, Gabriella, "William Lyon Mackenzie and the 1837 Rebellion," pamphlet at Mackenzie House, Toronto, undated.

Dent, John, Charles, *The Story of the Upper Canadian Rebellion.* Toronto: C.B. Robinson, 1885.

DCB: Dictionary of Canadian Biography: entries on various individuals.

Donnelly, F.K., "The British Background of William Lyon Mackenzie," *British Journal of Canadian Studies*, Vol. 2, No. 1, 1987, pp. 61–73.

Doughty, Arthur G., and Storey, Norah, editors, *Documents Relating to the Constitutional History of Canada, 1819–28*. Ottawa: J.O. Patenaude, printer to the King, 1935.

Dunham, Aileen, *Political Unrest in Upper Canada, 1815–36*. Toronto: McClelland and Stewart Limited, 1963.

Ellis, P. Berresford, and Mac A'Ghobhain, Seumas, *The Scottish Insurrection of 1820*, London: Victor Gollancz Ltd, 1970.

Fairley, Margaret, editor, *The Selected Writings of William Lyon Mackenzie 1824–37*. Toronto: Oxford University Press, 1960.

Flint, David, *William Lyon Mackenzie, Rebel Against Authority*. Toronto: Oxford University Press, 1971.

Fraser, John, *Eminent Canadians: Candid Tales of Now and Then*. Toronto: McClelland and Stewart, 2000.

Gates, Lillian F., *After the Rebellion. The Later Years of William Lyon Mackenzie*, Dundurn Press, 1988.

——. "The Decided Policy of William Lyon Mackenzie," *Canadian Historical Review*, 1959, Vol. 40, pp. 185–208.

Guillet, Edwin Clarence, *Early Life in Upper Canada*. Toronto: University of Toronto Press, 1933.

——. *Pioneer Days in Upper Canada*. Toronto: University of Toronto Press, 1963.

——. *The Great Migration: The Atlantic Crossing by Sailing Ship Since 1770*. Toronto: University of Toronto Press, 1937.

——. *The Life and Times of the Patriots: An Account of the Rebellion in Upper Canada*. Toronto: University of Toronto Press, 1968.

Hall, Roger, and Westfall, William, and Sefton, Laura, editors, *Patterns of the Past: interpreting Ontario history*. Toronto:

Dundurn Press, 1988.

Havel, Vaclav, *Disturbing the Peace*. Toronto: Vintage Books, 1991.

——. *Summer Meditations*. Toronto: Alfred A. Knopf Canada, 1992.

Head, Sir Francis Bond, *A Narrative with Notes by William Lyon Mackenzie*, edited by S. F, Wise. Toronto: McClelland and Stewart Limited, 1969.

Henderson, J.L.H. editor, *John Strachan: Documents and Opinions*. Toronto: McClelland and Stewart, 1969.

Hume, Fred Coyne, "The Reform Movement in Upper Canada," in *Profiles of a Province, Studies in the History of Ontario Commissioned by the Ontario Historical Society*. Toronto: Historical Society, 1967.

Jackson, Eric, "The Organization of Upper Canada Reformers, 1818–67." *Ontario History*, Vol LIII (1961), pp. 99–121.

Keilty, Greg, editor, *1837: Revolution in Canada As Told by William Lyon Mackenzie*, Toronto: N.C. Press, 1974.

Kilbourn, William, *The Firebrand*. Toronto: Irwin Publishing, 1956.

——, editor, *The Toronto Book*. Toronto: The MacMillan Company of Canada, 1976.

LeSeuer, William, *William Lyon Mackenzie: A Reinterpretation*. Toronto: Oxford University Press, 1971.

Lindsey, Charles, *The Life and Times of William Lyon Mackenzie*. Toronto: Randall, 1862 (only available on Microfiche at University of Toronto Library, CIHM 36386).

——. *William Lyon Mackenzie*. Toronto: Morang and Co., Limited, 1908.

Loenen, Nick, *Citizenship and Democracy: A Case for Proportional Representation*. Toronto: Dundurn Press, 1997.

Luno, Nancy, "A Genteel Exterior: The Domestic Life of William Lyon Mackenzie." Toronto: Toronto Historical Board, 1990, revised, 1999.

Mackay, R. A., "The Political Ideas of William Lyon Mackenzie,"
  CJEPS. February 1937, Vol. III, No. 1, pp. 1–22.
Macpherson, C.B., *The Real World of Democracy,* The Massey Lectures,
  Fourth Series. Toronto: Canadian Broadcasting Corporation
  Publication, 1965.
Milani, Lois Darroch, *Robert Gourlay, Gadfly.* Toronto: Ampersand
  Press, 1971.
Millar, A.H., *The Dundee Advertiser 1801–1901, A Centenary Memoir.*
  Dundee: Dundee Advertiser, 1901.

Newcome, Olive, *Picturesque Dundas Revisited.* Dundas, Ont.: Dundas
  Historical Society Museum, 1996.
Noel, S.J.R., *Patrons, Clients, Brokers: Ontario Society and Politics,*
  1791–1896. Toronto: University of Toronto Press, 1990.

Ogilvy, Graham, "The Radical Toun" in *The Dundee Book: An*
  Anthology of Living in the City edited by Billy Kay. Edinburgh:
  Mainstream, 1990.

Patterson, Graeme, "An Enduring Canadian Myth: Responsible
  Government and the Family Compact," in *Historical Essays on*
  Upper Canada: New Perspectives, edited by J.K. Johnson and
  Bruce G. Wilson. Ottawa, Carleton University Press, 1989.

Rae, K.D., "An Upper Canada Letter of 1829 on Responsible
  Government," *Canadian Historical Review,* Vol. 31, 1950.
Raible, Chris, "W.L. Mackenzie, Printer; His Newspapers and His
  Presses," pamphlet at Mackenzie House, Toronto, 1992.
——. *Muddy York Mud, Scandal & Scurrility in Upper Canada.* Dundurn
  Press, 1992.
——. *The Colonial Advocate: The Launching of the Newspaper and the*
  Queenston Career of William Lyon Mackenzie. Creemore, Ont:
  Curiosity House, 1999.

Rasporich, Anthony W., *William Lyon Mackenzie*. "Canadian History
     Through the Press Series." Toronto: Holt, Rinehart & Winston of
     Canada, Ltd., 1972.

Rea, J.E., "Barnabas Bidwell," *Ontario History*, Vol. 60, 1968.

——. "William Lyon Mackenzie—Jacksonian?" in J.M. Bumsted,
     Canadian History Before Confederation, 1979, p. 375.

Read , Colin and Stagg, Ronald J., editors, *The Rebellion of 1837 in
     Upper Canada: A Collection of Documents*. Toronto: Champlain
     Society in cooperation with the Ontario Heritage Foundation, 1985.

Rebick, Judy, *Imagine Democracy*. Toronto: Stoddart, 2000.

Romney, Paul, "A Struggle for Authority," in Russell's *Forging A
     Consensus*, pp. 10–40.

——. "William Lyon Mackenzie as Mayor of Toronto," *Canadian
     Historical Review*, Vol. 46, 1975, pp. 416–436.

Russell, Victor Loring, *Mayors of Toronto, Volume One, 1834–99*. Erin,
     Ontario: The Boston Mills Press, 1982.

——. editor, *Forging a Consensus: Historical Essays on Toronto*. Toronto:
     University of Toronto Press, 1984.

Salutin, Rick, and Theatre Passe Muraille, *1837: A History, A Play*.
     Toronto: James Lorimer & Company, 1976.

Schlesinger, Arthur M., Jr., *The Age of Jackson*. New York: Little Brown,
     1949.

Schrag, Peter, *Paradise Lost: California's Experience, America's Future*.
     New York: The New Press, 1998.

Select Committee on Grievances, Seventh Report, 1835. Legislative
     Assembly, Upper Canada (United Church Archives, Victoria
     University).

Tennant, Charles, *The Radical Laird: A Biography of George Kinloch,
     1775–1833*, Kineton: The Roundwood Press, 1970.

Thompson, E.P., *The Making of the English Working Class*, Penguin
     Books, 1968.

Wallace, W. Stewart, *The Family Compact*. Toronto: Glasgow, Brook, 1922.

Whatley, Christopher A., *Scottish Society, 1707–1830*. Manchester and New York: Manchester University Press, 2000.

——, and Swifen, David B., and Smith, Annette M., *The Life and Times of Dundee*. Edinburgh: J. Donald Publishers, 1993.

Wilton, Carol, *Popular Politics and Political Culture, 1800–1850*. Montreal: McGill-Queen's University Press, 2000.

Canadian Archives consulted

Dundas Historical Society Museum, Dundas, Ontario—Lesslie papers.

Ontario Archives, Grenville Street, Toronto—Mackenzie papers.

Index

Alien Question (Naturalization Act), 70-71, 93
Anderson, Anthony, 154
Arthur, Sir George, 161

Baldwin, Robert, 50, 69, 71, 93, 129, 155, 156
Baldwin, William, 69, 71
Bidwell, Barnabas, 69
Bidwell, Marshall, 46, 48, 61, 69, 71, 79, 93, 121
Bill 25, 188
Black Dwarf, 18
Boulton, Henry, 51, 95, 98, 102, 103
Boulton, James, 144
Brown, George, 173, 174, 176, 177, 178

Campbell, Justice William, 56, 61

Canada Company, 122, 125

Canadian Alliance Society, 118-119

Case, A.N., 174

Cato Street conspiracy, 23

Charles, Prince, 16, 28

Clark, John, 68

Clergy Reserves, 45, 77, 93, 119, 150, 173

Cobbett, William, 16, 18, 21, 30-37, 46, 102

Colbourne, Sir John, 88, 103, 104, 123, 125, 129

Colonial Advocate
    content, 44-47
    paper supply, 58
    Patrick Swift satires, 59-60
    postal problems, 58
    purpose, 42
    subscriptions, 43
    theft of type, 60

Constitutional Reform Society, 130

Dalton, Thomas, 48

Darling, Thomas, 164

democracy, 10-11, 164-167, 180, 197, 203-205, 208-211

Doyle, William, 164

Duncombe, Charles, 164

Dundee, 14, 17, 18, 21, 22, 26, 28, 29, 102, 177

Dundee, Perth and Cupar Advertiser, 18, 19

Dundee Rational Institution 19, 21

Durham, Lord 81, 169, 173

Edinburgh Review, 18, 20, 44

election reform, 90-91, 190-199

Everlasting Salary Bill, 90

Executive Council, 49, 80-82, 87, 103, 126, 129-130, 189

Family Compact, 16, 48-56, 59-61, 68, 79, 82, 88, 98, 119, 122, 145, 208

— as thirty tyrants, 55

Fitzgibbon, James, 157

Fletcher, Silas, 144, 159, 164

Glasgow, 23-26

Glenelg, Lord, 160

Goderich, Lord, 100, 103, 123

Gorham, Nelson, 144, 164

Gourlay, Robert, 65-69, 70, 93

Graham, Adam, 164

Grievances Committee, 121-129, 130, 142, 164

Gurnett, George, 146

Hagerman, Christopher Alexander, 53, 98, 102, 103

Hamilton, Robert, 68

Havel, Vaclav, 12, 190, 206

Hawk, John, 164

Hazlitt, William, 36

Head, Francis Bond, 129-132, 134, 141, 146, 155-161, 164-167, 191

Hunt, Henry, 16, 21, 66

Jackson, Andrew, 72, 83

Jarvis, Samuel, 60-61, 116, 156

Jefferson, Thomas, 72

Jeffrey, Francis, 20, 43

Kerr, William J., 68

Ketchum, Jesse, 69, 71, 77, 88

Kinloch, George, 22, 26, 28, 37, 66

Lee, Dennis, 9–10

Legislative Assembly, 45, 48-49, 57, 62-65, 78-79, 82, 86-90, 102-105,

125, 128, 130, 186, 188
Legislative Council, 45, 49, 64, 79-81, 83, 86, 87, 103, 125-126, 131, 189
Lesslie, James, 21, 41, 175, 177
Lindsey, Charles, 8, 14, 26, 35, 83, 98
Lloyd, Jesse, 144, 159, 164
Lonsdale, William Lowther, first and second earls, 27
Lount, Samuel, 8, 55, 144, 153, 155-157, 159-160, 164, 177

Macaulay, James B., 53, 59
Macdonald, Archibald, 154
Mackenzie, William Lyon
    Alien Question (Naturalization Act), 70
    American citizenship, 36, 170
    arriving in Canada, 39-40
    beaten by thugs, 99
    candidate for Assembly, 63, 75-76, 132, 174-75, 177
    children, 8, 41, 56-57, 60, 83, 99, 168, 170-172, 177
    democracy, 72, 167, 208-209
    death, 178
    description of society, 135–137
    early life, 14–15
    ejections from Assembly, 94-98, 102-105
    elected officials, 72-74, 86, 107-108
    election reform, 90-91
    escape, 159-160
    first hand experience, 92
    immigrants at Quebec, 91-92
    importance of public debate, 19, 47-48, 111-112, 134-135, 184-185
    informing the public, 39, 74, 96, 111, 180-181, 183
    issues, 76-77, 85-86
    'Justice shall reign', 137, 141
    'kept' newspapers, 42-43, 47
    libertine life, 26–27

London, 99–100
mayor, 112-118
member of Assembly, 78-80, 86, 89, 175-177
mother Elizabeth, 14, 41, 60, 169
moving to York, 57
names he was called, 9, 68, 88, 98
people the patron, 42
petition, 187, 197
political parties, 86-87
publisher, 44
rebellion broadsheet, 145–152
return to Upper Canada, 1849, 172
reward for, 159
shifting political views, 31
trial and imprisonment, 168-169
union of Upper and Lower Canada, 176
wife Isabel, 41, 56, 99, 167
wig, 10
MacNab, Allan, 88-89, 95, 157
Maitland, Sir Peregrine, 45, 59-60
Matthews, Captain John, 69
Matthews, Peter, 8, 55, 144, 157, 160
McKinnon, Ronald, 174-175
Montgomery, John, 168-169
Montgomery's Tavern, 153-157, 168
Moodie, Robert, 154
Morrison, T. D., 144
municipal reform, 109-111, 113-114

Nichol, Robert, 70

Papineau, Louis-Joseph, 143
Perry, Peter, 69
Peterloo, 22

political parties, 87, 188-190
Powell, Alderman John, 154

Radical(s), 17, 18, 22, 24, 25, 32, 37, 66
Randall, Robert, 42, 68, 71
Rebellion Losses Bill, 172
Reform(ers), 69, 79-80, 83, 87-90, 109-111, 114, 117-119, 122, 130-132, 137, 142, 144, 155
responsible government, 50, 134, 180
Rintoul, Robert Stephen, 18-20, 30, 102
Robinson, John Beverly, 52, 67-68
Rochefoucault-Liancourt, Duc de la, 27–28, 44
Roe, William, 77
Rolph, John, 69, 79, 129, 144, 152-157
Ryerson, Egerton, 93, 101-102, 132
Russell, Lord, 134

Sheppard, Joseph, 146, 152
Sidmouth, Lord, 23
Simcoe, John Graves, 40, 58
Stanley, Lord, 103-104
Strachan, John, 46, 49, 54, 59, 116, 122

Thomson, Edward, 117, 133
Thorne, Richard, 88
Thorpe, Robert, 64
time allocation, 185-187
Types Riot, 59–60, 77

Upper Canada Gazette, 47

Van Buren, Martin, 167, 170-171
Van Egmond, Colonel Anthony, 155, 157, 160, 164

Washburn, Simon, 88
Weekes, William, 64
Welland Canal, 128, 174
Western Mercury, 42
Wideman, Ludwig, 157
Willcocks, Joseph, 64-65
Willis, Judge John, 71–72
Willson, David, 209

York in 1820, 40-41
    cholera epidemic, 116
    in 1824, 56-57
    in 1834, 108-109
    in 1850 (Toronto), 172-173

A Note About the Type

Like *Mackenzie: A Political Biography*, the type in which this book is set reconsiders the past in a new light. BODONI EGYPTIAN (1997), by the designer of this book, Nick Shinn, combines simple, neo-classical form and proportion (derived from the work of Bodoni) with a mono-line stroke weight that is, uniquely, the same for capitals and lower case. Egyptian typefaces, with their slab-serifs and industrial strength, were invented by Vincent Figgins in the early nineteenth century (when they also acquired their curious name). The genre again found favour in the 1920s and 30s (*Memphis* et al), with a greater range of weight.